# 90 Day Challenge

**SOLUTIONS**

90daysolutions.com

Cover design by Jim Gulnick
Cover beautification by Lisett Guevara
www.90daysolutions.com

Photography by Amer Chaudhry
South Jersey based photographer, available for assignments worldwide.
www.amer-fotografia.net

NEW JERSEY, U.S.A (2014)

ISBN: 978-0-9848000-9-4

Published by 90daysoulmate.com, LLC

Learn how you make your book in 90 days: 90daybook.com

# 90 Day Challenge

## How to get the results you want in just 90 days.

## A DAY-BY-DAY METHOD TO YOUR OWN SUCCESSFUL BUSINESS

**LISETT GUEVARA, MSIE**

**JIM GULNICK, MBA**

**SOULMATE**

90daysoulmate.com, LLC.

New Jersey, USA

4

# Contents

## INTRODUCTION: 90 Day Challenge

More than a book, this document will become a lifeline for your business. This is a manual, guide, and calendar with which you can establish a daily action plan with easy-to-use content, and apply it to your personal life and your organization.

When business owners understand how learning is a function of active creation that evolves and constantly adapts to environmental shifts, they start building successful businesses that address social, technological, cultural, political, and economic changes.

The challenges business owners face today demand higher levels of knowledge and action. People must be personally and professionally competent in order to manage the material, procedural, attitudinal, technological, and social aspects of business with a comprehensive vision.

Business owners must be able to communicate and collaborate, to put into action the knowledge of the political, regulatory, and technological environment that affects their business, and to have technical mastery of training and productivity.

Today, an entrepreneur creates growth in the market through experience and trial and error, because there is still a wide gap between the speed of change and the ability to adapt. Therefore, the survival of entrepreneurs may dramatically exclude those who do not take the path of knowledge management, **the way of the evolution of knowledge based on action.**

This book is a strong example of how we have combined knowledge from countless university courses with experience in the workforce to create a method of simple steps developed so you can apply that knowledge to your organization in a practical and comfortable way – and in just 90 days of directed action.

To better explain the concepts we will be dealing with, we'll talk about Knowledge Management, characterized as the discipline responsible for designing and implementing a system which aims to identify, capture, and share the knowledge held within a company so that it can be converted into value for the organization.

The flow of information and knowledge within an organization means that organizations, like individuals, handle tools, processes, functions and roles that must be constantly redefined in response to change.

A smart business or organization is defined as one that projects and consistently uses the tacit knowledge that sometimes lies hidden in people's consciousness, in their internal processes, and in conversations among members of the organization. Studies have shown that the creation of knowledge is primarily a social rather than an individual process, and its management needs to be controlled, administered and maintained by the organization.

When organizations become conscious of the value of the intrinsic knowledge that is generated in each process, person, and action, they become able to treat that knowledge as another resource, one which can be used in planning exercises, impact studies, evaluation and monitoring, self-protection, accumulation, and operation.

On the other hand, it is common in the networked society of more developed countries to admit that capital, labor, and land are no longer basic resources; and that knowledge and information are currently the mainstay of business activity and, more than anything else, a potential factor in internal and external changes to businesses.

We must ask whether knowledge sometimes comes to have relatively minor importance compared to the rest of the elements involved in the production process of an organization, both in the manufacture of goods and the provision of services, since it is difficult to imagine the development of capital and more elaborate forms of production without knowledge being the dominant force behind the evolution of these factors.

However, knowledge without action is a very expensive waste, and fails to capture the endless opportunities offered by the environment. This book is an engine of action, and is the necessary tool to implement the kind of ideas and projects that come to mind, but never get started or finished. <u>We invite you to put your knowledge into action.</u>

**One more thing…**

The human spirit wants to live, survive, and prosper. The earliest humans sought food for nourishment to satiate this mission. The brain created organized activity in tactical and strategic behaviors acted out by a diverse collection of mechanical processes harbored in the incredible body. The operations carried out led the human organism to achieve its goals and feel the emotional satisfaction of increasingly beneficial objectives.

You are the result of thousands of years of perfecting this goal driven activity — spiritual, mental, physical, and emotional systems working in harmony. Business is nonetheless amazing extension of these core concepts.

Early humans learned about exchange and specialization. A grunt and physical gesture about one organizing the cave in return for the other hunting game or gathering provisions. More sophisticated bargaining included one building a shelter in return for the other digging an irrigation ditch. People learned what they were best at doing and traded their unique products and services for the products and services of others.

As trade became more complicated, a means of exchange that allowed storage of value and standardization became important. Money, clams, jewels, or some other third resource enabled economic growth. Beyond that, specialization within specializations occurred. The beam splitter, hole digger, and leaf layer became positions in the shelter building business. Water source tester, porosity specialist, and ground leveler became functions within the irrigation industry.

No matter how the business was organized the basics were the same — spirit, mental, physical, and emotional systems working in harmony. Or, at least that was the goal. The spirit of business is the mission and vision of the organization and also incorporates the values and culture, which are inherent. The mental qualities represent the organizational reporting structure, who is responsible for what, and the details of the strategy and tactics. The physical attributes envelop the equipment, processes, and functions that enable work to happen. Lastly, the emotions are the feelings contained within the company, the motivation and reward that urges successful delivery of customer solutions, and the satisfaction obtained as a result.

The point here is that the same influences that drive human struggle for survival are found in every organization. The same factors that impact creation and natural selection are part and parcel of a business. It is the act of embracing spiritual, mental, physical, and emotional dimensions that allow a synergistic approach to creating business strategies to survive and thrive in a given market amongst fierce competition.

Combine the knowledge you find in this book, the thoughts and strategies you create, and the experience you have to build a better business through the actions you select. You have infinite resources at your command and infinite possibilities at hand. Let your business be the conduit between those resources and possibilities and in it you will find limitless opportunities.

12

# CHAPTER 1 (Day 1)

## Starting the Challenge

The challenges may be different, but they have the common factor of being hard to achieve; they are goals that must be reached by overcoming various types of difficulties.

When we are faced with a challenge, the adrenaline in our body starts to move and generate a feeling of competence. But this competition is personal; it is fighting against our own limitations, against our own beliefs, seeking to establish actions that support a method and a discipline.

When we coach or advise our clients, the main values they establish are **discipline and commitment.** When there is no discipline or commitment, it is more difficult to succeed in challenges and projects, as many times it seems there is an initial enthusiasm, which fades as obstacles arise.

When one has the will to complete a project, and the discipline to know that the course involves both speed and endurance, one recognizes consciously that the path we are going to follow will bring many obstacles and difficulties that will be part of the process of learning we will establish in these 90 days.

This type of challenge can create temporary emotions, which can be dangerous if we do not have a clear idea of the goal we are headed for. The interesting thing about starting this type of challenge is that **you recognize yourself as being essentially an entrepreneur**. That is, you declare yourself to be a person that by his or her very nature has the ability to start towards and fight to achieve an established goal.

The beginning of this type of challenge requires that you have a defined vision of where you want to get to in your business, and it may be that at this time, that goal is not totally clear or there are limitations that prevent you from achieving it. The interesting thing about this guide is that it will allow you to adjust your focus towards the goal that will help you the most.

When a company or business is first started, people are charged with a passion that energizes each activity, and if these activities are well-planned and focused on one or more stated objectives, it will be easier to adjust the path to success and to conserve resources.

## What happens when you do not have a written plan?

The excitement of starting a business is sometimes like a blindfold for the owners, because they have all the information stored in their thoughts and in their hearts, and it would be very slow and boring to put all those wonderful ideas on paper.

This is where problems start, more so when you have business partners. Each one can have an open dialogue in which the objectives and principles of each partner are apparently aligned when discussed verbally; but when a critical situation occurs,

each one manages the values and goals differently and independently, making it difficult to establish a common area of action where everyone can see the big picture of the business in the same way.

Putting your objectives and a specific business plan down on paper will allow you to understand where you are now and, more importantly, where you are going.

Imagine that you have the plans for your home in your mind, and your partner and other family members do too. You all live under the same roof, but there comes a time when the family grows and must build a new room and an additional bathroom. Mentally, each person imagines a bathroom with a tub, shower, sink in different places, without considering the physical reality of the locations of the water inflow, water discharge, electricity, etc.

So, each one imagines the parts of the bathroom as different units in different places. This is explained to the construction worker who, with his experience, does the best he can, because he does not know the house plans.

This person will have to perform many excavations to find the services. Many resources of time, labor, money, and material will be lost by the exploration, and by trying to get the final work to satisfy each of the family members. It will be a very difficult task, indeed. The simple fact of establishing a written plan, like plans for a house, gives you and your partners an objective, specific, and clear understanding of where you are and where you want to go in the business world.

## Monitoring

Any plan that is not monitored becomes an uncontrolled open water valve, where you can lose all of this valuable resource. Monitoring should become part of the habit or routine to confirm that what you are doing is effective and goes towards the achievement of objectives.

If you are the type of person who begins many things, but completely finishes few of them or changes target after the first failure, this is the important moment when you will learn how to complete a project and recognize when you should stop striving and change your path, or keep fighting to the finish line along the same road.

That crossroads of being able to recognize whether to change or continue in the same way has been an arduous task for us. It is a struggle between the passion of what you want to do and always dreamed of doing, versus the reality of a market, an economy, or a business situation. Here we will offer the middle way, where you will not have to abandon your original dream, but can modify it to match the reality of the market in which you want to develop your business.

Monitoring is an effective discipline to assess, analyze, and make timely decisions in the face of situations that arise. It must become routine, establishing a common pattern in time, space, and quantities used to review and to create benchmarks.

For the 90-day process, you must establish a plan and schedule in which each day you will manage tasks to be evaluated and compared to the pattern established to demonstrate the project's progress.

For example, if in the second week you identify four activities to be undertaken that involve man-hours of work, it is important to measure how many man-hours are needed to accomplish the tasks as well as the daily percentage of compliance. At the end of the week you will follow up and determine whether the goal was completely achieved and whether more man-hours are required, and you may also compare the productivity of the previous week in similar activities.

As you can see, monitoring allows you to analyze each task and to adjust its initial plan, for this goes hand in hand with reality. This 90-day plan is not a straitjacket where you cannot get out of the initial plan. On the contrary, it permits you to adjust your strategies and resources, knowing that the entire project must be completed in 90 days, but that the monitoring you do each week will serve as a thermometer you can use to adjust your plans and move forward.

Every organization and person is different, but having this habit or discipline of planning and monitoring in any project will make you able to move the pieces that will allow you to complete the activities very closely to the way they were planned, and to manage resources in such a way that you achieve the ultimate goal.

## Why 90 days?

The reason it is 90 days, and not 60 or 120, is because it is always after 30 days that people who manage projects begin to really understand the performance of the activities and of the system, the behavior of the people, how the resources are managed, and how they are used. In the second month, or 60 days, you will be able to see the results of the adjustments you have made; and in the last month, you can add the resources necessary to complete the masterpiece.

This process has been tested in different areas, such as personal, employment, financial, family, health, etc. And this approach has permitted the achievement of goals and objectives by using a method.  The important thing here is to follow the method step-by-step, which will allow you to conserve the resources of opportunity, time, or money that you put into play when setting up a project.

There are many studies about the 90 days, and when it comes to nature, one can see that the seasons of spring, summer, winter and fall have that approximate duration.  At the same time, the seasons are where nature shows its ability to transform, to display itself, and to prepare for next season.

These natural cycles teach us fundamental principles that we must take into account during the process.

## Natural Principles

1.-   *The changes are part of the process and should be valued as learning tools.*
     ***"Adaptation"***

The ability to adapt to changes in the environment is one of the primary principles of nature.  The power to withstand changes in temperature, atmospheric conditions, and other stressors has been a real challenge for Mother Earth.  And despite the constant attack, she has managed to survive and keep offering the seasons with some variations, but she has never decided to close her business.

Nature values these changes and takes them as part of the evolutionary process.  Similarly, entrepreneurs must understand that changes and obstacles are part of business, and should appreciate and accept them.

2.- *A service or product can change its appearance or content as the business changes **without losing its essence.***

There is a fear of change that makes us believe that if we change we may lose the essence of the business. That fear has caused many organizations to become frozen, and to die before seeing the possibility of making changes without completely losing their original identity.

When you understand the essence of the business very clearly, while you can give it certain shades of agreement with the environment in order to survive, it is not necessary to lose the project or your original passion. This is like the mimicry of the chameleon, which changes color depending on the circumstances, but will always be a chameleon, which has only changed color to seize an opportunity or to protect itself.

3.- *The fact that an element of the business is not working does not mean that the whole business does not work. **"Temporality"***

When a tree loses all its leaves because of the arrival of autumn, it does not mean that we should remove it, as it is preparing for the winter; the tree must support the weight of the snow without its trunk dying or collapsing. And after the winter passes, the new leaves will start to grow.

This example reflects actions taken in business when a process or product is eliminated, when an element of the organization is removed or disappears for the simple reason that it is not the same as it used to be, or is not giving the expected result. It is important for businesses to recognize which elements are right for the times, and which are not; and to recognize what to keep, what to modify, and what to eliminate.

*4.- There are times to invest, to save, to drive, to grow the business. We must know the **business cycles** and understand that not all periods are equal.*

It is very important to know the cycles of the market, and of your business. Every business has its season, has its behavior over time, and in knowing this you will understand when it's time to save, to produce, or to go out and sell, and promote your business. Not all times are equal, and if you are not aware of this principle you can lose time, money, and opportunities.

*5.- Have **the perseverance to persist, with the patience to wait** for activities to be successful.*

The perseverance to persist and the patience to wait seem to contradict each other, but this is a fundamental factor of business. Persistence has always been a success value; but when we look at the growth of a plant, it requires constant watering and daily care, but we cannot say *hurry, grow fast*. We must have the patience to marvel each day at the tiny amount of progress it has made.

Business works the same way. You must be persistent and patient; and you should marvel at each minimal daily advance in the activities you undertake and the successes you achieve. There is no final plant size, nor is there a final size for your business.

*6.- Recognize the **natural risks** of the business and how to accept and prevent them.*

There are unavoidable natural risks. The most important thing is to identify them, create a plan to prevent them, and find ways to minimize their impact, and even in some cases to eliminate them.

Intelligent and methodical risk management greatly helps organizations to survive damage that could otherwise be fatal.

The same thing occurs in nature, where we know the risks that flora, fauna, and human beings may all be subject to, but that does not stop us from taking action and preventing these dangers.

7.-   *Monitor and **follow up** on an objective and routine approach.*

The perseverance to persist, which we discussed in the fifth principle, should be measured and controlled as we may be digging a hole in a place where it is not appropriate; and we may have patience directed without measure and control, which can waste our resources without any benefit down the road. It is important to accompany these principles with clear objectives and under a controlled monitoring pattern that allows us to determine whether our efforts are well directed.

8.-   ***Continuous improvement** is a value that is infinite within infinite resources and opportunities.*

Belief in continuous improvement allows us to see the opportunities for improvement in each situation; it enables the lens with which we view the environment to perceive the infinity of resources we possess. Just as nature knows that it can take many resources from the earth to evolve different species and that they will adapt and transform themselves in the process of evolution or continuous improvement, you must also understand that there is always a better path and a better way of doing things; and that this offers endless possibilities to achieve, according to the concept that there are infinite resources on earth.

## 90-DAY AGENDA

For the agenda, you need to plan your week, day by day, in your personal or electronic calendar, or if you prefer, you can use the form at the end of this chapter.

The important thing for the development of the agenda is to keep in mind that it must be done by keeping records, whether in digital or paper form, and by following up. This book is structured in a way that makes it easy for you to schedule your activities as you read each chapter.

You have two ways to work with this book. One is that as you read the book, chapter-by-chapter, you complete the exercises when they appear, finishing with the days indicated in the index. The other is to read all of the material; after the end of each chapter, write your list of things to do "**List of Activities**" and then proceed to fill out the form "**90-day plan**". These two forms may be used chapter by chapter, and will create a record of what you have to do and when you have to do it.

We also include a weekly monitoring aid that allows you to have better control and permits you to determine where you are losing time, and where productivity problems exist called the **"Weekly Productivity Plan"**.

*90 Day Challenge*

## List of Activities

In this document, you will take note by chapter of each activity that you think must be undertaken to achieve the established objective. Besides allowing you to establish your priorities, whether high or low, it will then be easier to establish an order in the weekly plan and the 90-day plan. This list can be modified as you read the book, and especially as you write down information on **90-day Plan** about your planned activities. It allows you to add, delete and/or modify activities at the same time as you plan them.

## 90-day Plan

The plan is designed for each day, and you will write down your observations of the case as you carry out the activities. As mentioned above, this plan can be modified and is adaptable to your time constraints. When you do the analysis of its execution **Weekly Productivity Plan**, this will allow you to better manage your resources and to administer them in the best way to achieve your ultimate goal in 90 days.

## Weekly Productivity Plan

This document allows you to measure what was planned versus what was done, and to analyze why established activities have not been completed.

Fill out your scheduled activities on Sunday leading into the week being planned using this form, where each activity of the following five days is established. Every night, you should review what has been done and focus on what could not be done. Analyze the cause and reschedule incomplete activities for the next day. You may end up loading the next day with more activities, since the planned target was not met.

Try not to go astray in the first week, because often we are ambitious and plan many activities without knowing our ability to respond; and possibly when activities depend not only on you but another person, they may be more difficult to complete.

This weekly discipline will train you to get to know your own skills better, to improve them, and in turn will minimize your "not done" list in the second or third week. Our experience, and the statistics of clients that have used this method, show that week four is the time when the rhythm of the plan becomes more certain and productivity begins to increase. In other words, expect some bumps in the road before finding smooth pavement.

You can see that we set a very demanding schedule, starting from seven in the morning and ending late. The simple reason for this tight schedule is that if you want to have your own productive business in 90 days, you must invest a lot of money and time. And it is up to you to decide whether to spend the money to hire people to perform certain activities and delegate so that you have a more comfortable time, or to sacrifice 90 days of your own hard work and training to achieve the target. You can choose to use the word invest rather than sacrifice.

Remember, only you know your business, only you have the ideas and creativity in your mind, only you have the challenge of achieving your goal, your project. And all of that requires extra effort. Ask some great, successful business people if the start of their enterprises was comfortable and quiet

## LIST OF ACTIVITIES

| CHAPTER | ACTIVITY | HIGH | LOW |
|---|---|---|---|
| | | | |
| | | | |
| | | | |
| | | | |
| | | | |
| | | | |
| | | | |
| | | | |
| | | | |
| | | | |
| | | | |
| | | | |
| | | | |
| | | | |
| | | | |
| | | | |
| | | | |
| | | | |
| | | | |
| | | | |

## 90-DAY PLAN

| DAY | DATE | ACTIVITY | RESPONSIBLE | NOTE |
|-----|------|----------|-------------|------|
|     |      |          |             |      |
|     |      |          |             |      |
|     |      |          |             |      |
|     |      |          |             |      |
|     |      |          |             |      |
|     |      |          |             |      |
|     |      |          |             |      |
|     |      |          |             |      |
|     |      |          |             |      |
|     |      |          |             |      |
|     |      |          |             |      |
|     |      |          |             |      |
|     |      |          |             |      |
|     |      |          |             |      |
|     |      |          |             |      |
|     |      |          |             |      |
|     |      |          |             |      |
|     |      |          |             |      |
|     |      |          |             |      |
|     |      |          |             |      |
|     |      |          |             |      |
|     |      |          |             |      |

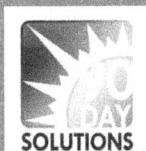

## WEEKLY PRODUCTIVITY PLAN

| MONDAY | PLAN | NOT DO | BECAUSE |
|---|---|---|---|
| 7:00 AM | | | |
| 8:00 AM | | | |
| 9:00 AM | | | |
| 10:00 AM | | | |
| 11:00 AM | | | |
| 12:00 M | | | |
| 1:00 PM | | | |
| 2:00 PM | | | |
| 3:00 PM | | | |
| 4:00 PM | | | |
| 5:00 PM | | | |
| 6:00 PM | | | |
| 7:00 PM | | | |
| 8:00 PM | | | |
| TUESDAY | PLAN | NOT DO | BECAUSE |
| 7:00 AM | | | |
| 8:00 AM | | | |
| 9:00 AM | | | |
| 10:00 AM | | | |
| 11:00 AM | | | |
| 12:00 M | | | |
| 1:00 PM | | | |
| 2:00 PM | | | |
| 3:00 PM | | | |
| 4:00 PM | | | |
| 5:00 PM | | | |
| 6:00 PM | | | |
| 7:00 PM | | | |
| 8:00 PM | | | |

# WEEKLY PRODUCTIVITY PLAN

| WEDNESDAY | PLAN | NOT DO | BECAUSE |
|---|---|---|---|
| 7:00 AM | | | |
| 8:00 AM | | | |
| 9:00 AM | | | |
| 10:00 AM | | | |
| 11:00 AM | | | |
| 12:00 M | | | |
| 1:00 PM | | | |
| 2:00 PM | | | |
| 3:00 PM | | | |
| 4:00 PM | | | |
| 5:00 PM | | | |
| 6:00 PM | | | |
| 7:00 PM | | | |
| 8:00 PM | | | |
| THURSDAY | PLAN | NOT DO | BECAUSE |
| 7:00 AM | | | |
| 8:00 AM | | | |
| 9:00 AM | | | |
| 10:00 AM | | | |
| 11:00 AM | | | |
| 12:00 M | | | |
| 1:00 PM | | | |
| 2:00 PM | | | |
| 3:00 PM | | | |
| 4:00 PM | | | |
| 5:00 PM | | | |
| 6:00 PM | | | |
| 7:00 PM | | | |
| 8:00 PM | | | |

# WEEKLY PRODUCTIVITY PLAN

| FRIDAY | PLAN | NOT DO | BECAUSE |
|---|---|---|---|
| 7:00 AM | | | |
| 8:00 AM | | | |
| 9:00 AM | | | |
| 10:00 AM | | | |
| 11:00 AM | | | |
| 12:00 M | | | |
| 1:00 PM | | | |
| 2:00 PM | | | |
| 3:00 PM | | | |
| 4:00 PM | | | |
| 5:00 PM | | | |
| 6:00 PM | | | |
| 7:00 PM | | | |
| 8:00 PM | | | |
| SATURDAY | PLAN | NOT DO | BECAUSE |
| 7:00 AM | | | |
| 8:00 AM | | | |
| 9:00 AM | | | |
| 10:00 AM | | | |
| 11:00 AM | | | |
| 12:00 M | | | |
| 1:00 PM | | | |
| 2:00 PM | | | |
| 3:00 PM | | | |
| 4:00 PM | | | |
| 5:00 PM | | | |
| 6:00 PM | | | |
| 7:00 PM | | | |
| 8:00 PM | | | |

## CHAPTER 2 (Day 2)

## Design Your Mission, Vision, and Goals

In this section, you can establish one of the first steps required to establish your business. On many occasions, people have ideas to create a business but cannot figure out how to start; others have already begun, but have not established order and feel they have no control.

In both cases, this tool is a step-by-step guide towards making that connection between what is in the mind and heart of the leader, in addition to providing effective actions to create a thriving business.

Human beings can think, imagine, and dream about what they want and then make it happen, but if we do not have tools to help us to realize these thoughts methodically and productively, we suffer the consequences of living in a dream that becomes a nightmare.

This tool easily provides the necessary actions so that the thrilling ideas in your mind can be projected and brought into reality.

Like many others, you may have happened to think of the "perfect business", which you imagined when you saw a need in the market, a product or service that is not being marketed, and you thought it should be a success. But the months or days pass, and then you bump into someone who did it, and you say: *"I thought about that myself..."* Yes, but you took no action.

Perhaps you did not take action because you did not have the tools, the courage, the time or the money. These are all excuses from now on, because with this information you will realize that there are no limitations in starting a business. All the limitations are in your mind.

First we must know what you really came to do on this planet. What is your mission in life? Do you know what your talents and abilities are? Do you know what your passion is?

These questions seem easy, but we must devote the necessary time to them, so that you can connect what you are currently doing with what you want to do.

Many people have ended up in their own businesses for various reasons. In some cases it was inherited, they were presented with an unexpected opportunity, or someone invited them and they found it interesting to join the project, etc. But there is another group that always had a dream, had in their minds and hearts the hope of doing something that they loved, something they found exciting, and something they knew was their mission in life.

We will provide some tips on how to connect what you have inside with what your organization does or is required to do:

1. What talents, skills, and knowledge do you possess?
2. What specific things do you love to do?

3. How do your talents, skills, and knowledge relate to your passion?

4. What do you believe you came to this planet to do?

5. What do you want to do in your company or project?

6. What are your personal and business needs?

7. What are your personal and business values?

8. How are your values positively or negatively related to your needs?

Before answering each question, it is important to understand the elements that are used in this exercise. We will explain in more detail, so that you can do an excellent job of analysis and documentation. Once you have developed the answers to these questions, you will be able to have a clearer picture, and you will know whether or not your life mission can fit your business mission.

Remember something very important: when movie heroes must fulfill their missions, they are never discouraged, they never tire, they do not complain, they do not protest; there are no excuses or obstacles that they cannot deal with in order to fulfill their missions. And while they are confronting problems and fighting enemies, every obstacle becomes an adventure in which the hero does not give up on achieving his goal.

We invite you to discover your life mission. Put on your superhero cape to connect with yourself, and you can achieve everything you desire.

## 1. What talents, skills, and knowledge do you possess?

It is important to know the difference between these elements, because while they may look similar, they are not. Knowledge is the fact of knowing something, and skill is the ability to do it.

When we speak of knowledge, we refer to theoretical information acquired about a subject, whether it is information learned through reading, training, or any other form of education.

On the other hand, skills are the practical ability to apply the knowledge gained. In some cases skills may be innate, as there are people who have developed skills without studying previously, perhaps by watching or simply making an attempt using trial and error, and have thus developed a specific skill.

When it comes to talent, we can say it is a combination of the two definitions, where the capacity of a person to understand how to resolve situations in an intelligent way is combined with their own abilities, skills, knowledge, experience, and aptitudes.

Being able to describe every talent, skill, and knowledge you possess in clear terms will give you the basics needed to better know yourself and to understand the tools you have.

Be aware of the importance of this part of your self-analysis, since a lack of knowledge or awareness of the skills we have can make the road more difficult to navigate. And when we know who we really are, we can better understand our own strengths and weaknesses. In this way, you can identify areas that need improvement and those you can take advantage of more easily.

Imagine a person who has stage fright and is afraid of public speaking, but wishes to be a famous author, as the person has many good ideas and does not need to deal with large groups to write books. That's fine, but when it comes time to sell the book, one of the techniques is through seminars, workshops, conferences, etc. Then, that person has the option of developing a new talent or of hiring another person to do that activity.

With this example, we are not saying that the fact of not having specific knowledge and/or a certain skill will limit you in completing your project or life mission. What we want to explain is that by recognizing who you are, you will more clearly understand your advantages and disadvantages when it comes to establishing your mission in life.

When people recognize their talents, they can become superheroes more quickly and easily. Some people have an innate ability to connect with others when communicating, and they can sell just about anything because they have that gift that makes them unique when presenting a product or service. Such people can go far in the areas where they recognize their own abilities, because just knowing what talents they have and above all, believing in their own talents, gives them the potential they need to succeed.

A simple way to perform this analysis is to recall some activities in which you have easily succeeded, and where other people have recognized that you have performed very well.

Another way is to evaluate the knowledge gained during all the years you have lived, as well as the experience you have gained. There are people who have worked for twenty years as assistants or technicians in a machine shop and do not recognize all the knowledge they have in the mechanical or electrical areas, their knowledge of parts, the amount of training they have received, etc.

Evaluate yourself and be thorough in reviewing your entire path, both in knowledge and in talent, and design a comprehensive document that illustrates who you really are and what you really have. At the end of the chapter you can use the form **"Determine Your Skills"**.

## 2. What specific things do you love to do?

Recognizing the things we are passionate about is an interesting task. We will take you by the hand to discover the activity that moves the fiber of your being, the activity you can perform with excitement, focus and energy. We recommend, as with all the activities in this book, that you take notes, that you write, because through writing you can tap the wealth of information that you must organize and process in order to put it into action.

The best way to discover your passion is to answer the following questions:
- Which activity makes time pass so that you do not realize it?
- What would you be willing to do without being paid a cent?
- At this moment, what would you choose to do for the rest of your life?
- If you died and had the opportunity to return, what would you do?
- Which activities trigger your creativity and excite you?
- Recall moments when you do something that brings joy, makes you jump up and down, energizes you and brings you happiness.

Once you answer these questions honestly, you will be more focused on the path you want to follow. Take your time when answering these questions, because ideas will surface in your mind and can revive your passion.

## 3. How to relate your talents, skills, and knowledge to your passion.

In this step of the exercise it is important that you have written the answers to steps one and two, because now you need to relate your passion to your skills, talents and knowledge.

The best way to do this is to make a comparison chart where you list your knowledge, skills, abilities, talents, and the activities that thrill you. In this way, you will be able to connect what they have in common and what you can best use to turn your passion into action. Having a passion without taking action turns into frustration, and it does a lot of damage over the years if it is not fulfilled. So you see the importance of this activity to your personal life as well as your business, financial, family, and professional lives. Here you can discover what's happening in your life that is causing you not to succeed in what you really want.

You may be reading this book and looking at the exercises and thinking, *I don't have time to answer, let alone write the answers to this many questions; I need to solve my business problem, my financial problem.* Consequently, you do not follow the steps listed here, and later you might wonder why you are in the same place as before, why you do not advance in business.

Observe whether following instructions is a problem for you, since in most cases this is the greatest obstacle to improving any area of your life.

Notes:

_____

_____

_____

_____

Having identified the resources available to you when setting up a business is a priority, and one of the main resources is the business knowledge that you must establish. Imagine that you are going to install a laboratory for stem cells taken from the placentas of babies at birth, but you do not have the slightest idea of how to do this or what benefits it has, and you do not even like medicine. You are trying to develop something for which motivation and enthusiasm will not guarantee that you are on the right track, unless you are simply an investor in the business.

The analysis of this activity should highlight those cases that are related, and you must find out which passions have no relation to your talents. In this way you will either make the decision to work and develop new talent, or simply to dedicate yourself only to the activities that you are passionate about and for which you have the talent, knowledge, and skills.

You must be honest with yourself and not hide your conflicting activities, as this is where energy is dissipated and where lack of productivity demolishes projects, plans, and passions.

### 4. What do you believe you came to this planet to do?

It may seem a little strange to ask what you came to this planet to do, but this kind of question gives us the introspection to analyze our life mission, the reason and the cause for being here with the skills and talents we possess. In addition to the knowledge gained on the way, this mix of who you are and what your goal is opens doors in your mind through which you can see answers that are often very obvious, but cannot be seen.

Describe in detail the reason why you are here in this place, country, city, community where you belong, with the cargo of information and knowledge that you have.

Starting to write about this will allow you to take the first steps to identify your mission in life. And then you must link your mission in life to the mission of your business.

We will help you with some personal questions so that you have the foundation that will facilitate the realization of the organization's mission. You cannot disassociate the two missions because that will not allow you to understand the fundamental reason for the business you are establishing.

The following example will show you how to connect the information to create a mission for your organization.

In Lisett's case, she has a natural talent for negotiation; her passion for finding out how to proactively unite resources with needs makes her an expert negotiator. Additionally, she has trained for many years as an information engineer, with a master's degree in industrial engineering, which gives her the tools to manage information, processes, innovation, and technology, among others. Based on these elements and her passion for creating solutions, she established the company *90Daysolutions Llc*, which offers consulting services, training, and business reengineering. That mix of knowledge, skills, and experience means that her **life mission** combined with the mission of the organization work together for a common goal. And when we determine who we are working for, we open up opportunities to clearly see our potential customers.

Questions:

- What do we do well as people?
- What are we seeking with what we do?
- Where do we do it?
- Why do we do it?
- Who do we do it for?

Answering these questions in a personal manner allows you to combine this information with your business activities, and this is good because these same questions will later be applied to identify the mission of your business.

Your personal mission can be described in one or more phrases; in just answering these questions, you will recognize what your mission in life is, and what you came to do here on this planet.

Do not be surprised if in doing this exercise you discover new things, new ideas, and even new ways different from those you previously considered or have been using in your current business. This is the time to discover yourself and the talents you can put into action as a driving force to achieve your desired success.

Humans redesign themselves constantly; you can re-create, re-start yourself. Allow yourself the opportunity to start a new project, a new lifestyle, a new season, a refresh of your daily life. No matter how old you are, allow this change in your life, because we do not know what will happen in the next.

## 5.  What do you want to do in your company or project?

At this point, with all the personal details, we can focus the artillery on your business.  Does the project you are working on, or the company where you are working, allow you to fulfill your mission in life?

The company for which you want to develop a mission and vision must have the service and/or product it offers identified.  No matter what type of organization you have, the important thing is to specifically describe what it is dedicated to, and then you will be able to determine what it does in comparison with what it wants to do.

The mission of an organization is a public announcement, which should be visible to everyone and especially kept in view of the owners of the organization, its employees, its customers, its suppliers, and the general public.

It is this flag that symbolizes power, choice, clarity, focus, direction, order, and why not say it, the feeling of defiance, of challenges.  It is the announcement to the entire world that we know who we are and where we are going.

When organizations know, understand, feel, breathe, and vibrate recognizing who they are and where they are going, the energy that moves them is much better, and their productivity is shown by the facts.

### Develop your business mission.

To design the mission of the organization, you must simply answer the same questions as in point four, but with a focus on your business or project.

Below, we pose these questions again with a business approach, so that you may describe the mission of the company. The wording of a mission statement has been a topic of discussion for many years among business consultants, business owners, auditors, etc. But the way you draw it up is not important here; what matters is the information it contains. This is why we recommend that you write it with the information we have asked, and another important point is its publication.

Questions:

- What do we do well as a company?
- What are we seeking with what we do?
- Where do we do it?
- Why do we do it?
- Who do we do it for?

You can find a lot of information on the internet about how to write a mission statement, but the bottom line here is that it contains clear information about what the company does, how it does it, why it does it, and for whom. This is the foundation for realizing the vision.

**Develop your business vision.**

When you were answering the questions above, you may have listed activities that you are not currently doing and that should wait a little longer to be implemented in your business plan, either in the medium or long term. That declaration of aspiration about what you envision and desire for your company's future is what you are going to develop into a business vision.

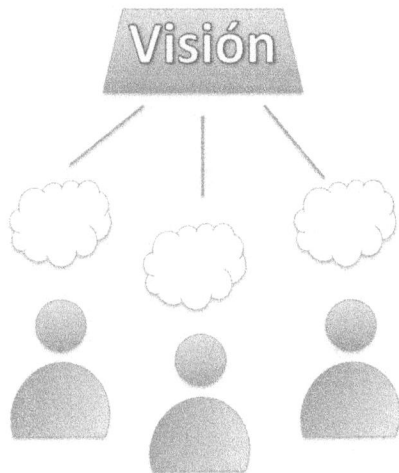

The important thing is to recognize and differentiate between what you are and do (mission) and what you want to be and want to do (vision). Putting these two statements together allows you to create a future plan. It is the ability to know where you stand and which way you will lead the organization.

Most things in life were first created mentally, then were visualized and put on paper, and finally created physically. The power to visualize becomes the strategy of creation for organizations. Creative visualization consists in having an image of what you want for the organization, and this image is recreated in the minds of the participants in the project or business. It is done in such a way that each person is involved in an exchange of ideas about how they want to project the organization into the future, and when they have all shared their input, it is captured on paper to make it easier to establish goals and plans to achieve them.

In designing the vision it is advisable to involve project members and other stakeholders, because the point of view of a third party often helps create fresh ideas that benefit the new vision of the organization.

Grounded with mission information that has already been developed, you can generate new ideas and help yourself with the following questions:
- What is the desired image of our business?
- How will we be in the future?
- What will we do in the future?

- What activities will we develop in the future?

Once you have established the mission and vision, it will be easier to establish the objectives and the organizational structure -- in short, what you want to do and who you are going to do it with.

## 6. What are your personal and business needs?

You have probably heard of Maslow's famous pyramid that describes the hierarchy of human needs. This pyramid is very simple and shows levels of needs ranging from basic to high-level. This scale has a logical reason to exist, and satisfying the needs at each level allows you to achieve the higher levels.

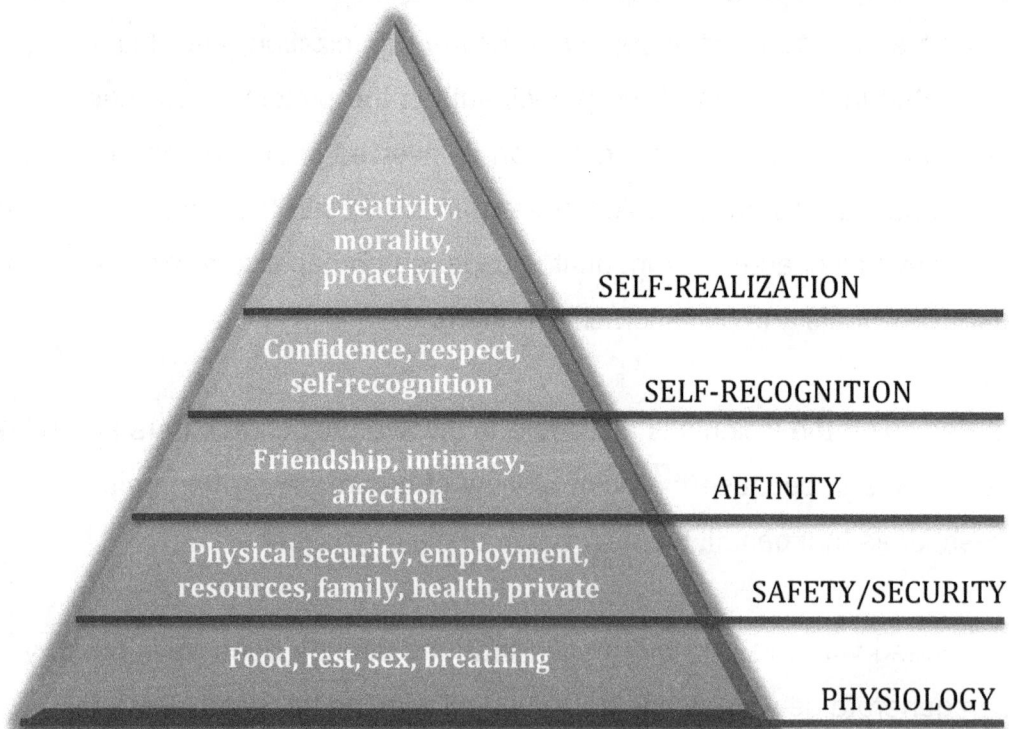

The hierarchy of needs is critical for understanding certain details that can derail your business, and even derail your 90-day project.

90 Day Challenge

If the basic needs of food, health, and safety are not covered, it is very difficult for human beings to generate new ideas, apply creativity, and take on major new challenges.

We have touched on this theory of the hierarchy of needs because we can use this classification to help you determine your personal needs and the needs of your business.

As you can see, all the information we are giving you is linked and has a logical sequence that allows you to establish a system with solid and sustainable foundations. Relating your personal mission to the mission of the organization lets you see you are walking down the right path, and linking your individual needs with business needs allows you to direct the path to the desired and necessary objectives.

Make a list of the personal needs that you have at this time; you can use the picture of the pyramid, where you can go from eating and resting, through security, affection, and trust, to reach self-actualization. Once you write the list, it is important that you arrange it based on your priorities, so that the items are in order from highest to lowest priority according to their importance.

Then make a list of the organization's needs, and similarly, list them from most to least important. Once both lists are complete, select the top three needs from both lists and check whether or not they are similar.

This exercise will show you whether there is affinity in terms of the needs of both areas so that you can determine whether the objectives that you must contemplate are going in the same direction.

*Needs* are responsible for *activating emotions* that can inspire or destroy a business. Emotions are an important factor that many entrepreneurs manage wisely, and give them a role in making decisions that can cause them to win or lose. When needs are aligned with values and do not contradict them, harmony appears and the forces of resistance are minimized.

## 7. What are your personal and business values?

Values exist in homes, families, and society, as well as in businesses and organizations. Values are fundamental beliefs that characterize human beings when they think, choose, and act at any given time. Values are the thermometer of our behavior, and form a pattern of behavior within each of our personal, family, social, and work circles. When values are clearly defined and established, it is easier to understand the causes and reasons for people's behavior in any situation.

There are people who are so grounded in their values that their decisions are based purely on the pattern of their beliefs, whether or not those decisions are beneficial for themselves or their environment. That pattern is the lens through which you see the world and through which your interpretation of the world will also be based.

In organizations, values have been pillars that have sustained businesses for many years. There are companies that have very well-founded values despite conflicting values held by the society around them, or by their workers or employees, or by the country where the business is established. As long as the values are well-founded they may guarantee the integrity of the organization. It is amazing how we have known companies that have gone through economic, social, and political crises and have maintained strong values in order to be a center of transformation for persons belonging to the organization.

The point of this discussion is to understand that personal values are not contrary to organizational values. To simplify, we will present an example: let's assume that the members of an organization have the value of honesty as number one on their list of values, but have created an organization whose main customer is the government of a country where corruption levels are very high. When presenting their product or service to their unique customer, they must act in opposition to the principal value of the organization. At that moment, they must make the decision to change the focus of the company to the private sector where this value is not affected, because functioning in a manner contrary to the values of the organization will sooner or later destroy it.

You can see why it is in your best interests to establish a list of your personal values and your organizational values, and handle these in the same way as you did the needs. List the values in descending order, and compare the first three values in each list. In this way, you can observe and manage information so that both lists can operate in synchrony and not create conflicts, which we often think are simple but can become a silent enemy that eventually explode and destroy the organization or its members. That's when illnesses and stress arise, and the business becomes a disagreeable place where you feel obligated to be and where it is not pleasant to work.

## 8. How are your values positively or negatively related to your needs?

When making your lists of both values and needs, detailed analysis is required to establish whether any of your personal or organizational needs connect in a positive or negative way with the values.

48

Let's start with the values and what we will call anti-values. This refers to those values that were programmed into our minds and our beliefs in a positive way, but the way they have been interpreted has generated a negative aspect that allows them to be called anti-values.

To better explain the point we present the following example: when a father and mother tell their children that *"big boys don't cry"*, with this they are seeking to form a value of strength, of having the maturity to face things in a brave way, but at the same time this phrase expresses a limitation of feelings and emotions. Consequently, these children connect in their minds that the fact of expressing their emotions makes them weak, and then they close up and will not share their feelings and experiences, blocking an emotional area; and they think that the less they feel, the better.

It is therefore important to examine the values we have created in our minds and our organizations with phrases that can be interpreted negatively, which may in turn lead to conflicts with the needs of the organization or its members.

There are values that can falter in the presence of some needs; and that's where this chapter of the book seeks to make a great contribution to the reader, because a business owner may have strong values based on not asking for help, not accepting cash or credit, but the organization needs funding to continue operating. This is where the values should be revised, because as an organizational objective the company must generate revenues and profits, and this sort of value may be blocking the progress of the organization in some cases, or may be taking care of or protecting the organization in other cases.

This is a very interesting and delicate area where with the help of developed documents, analysis meetings, and interpretation, you can understand which aspects are holding back the growth of your organization or placing it at risk.

In the following table, it is important to note that the mission, vision, and values all need to be reviewed in a personal and organizational manner in order to set clear and achievable targets.

## GOALS

Goal setting is a key task in which we must consider certain basic premises in order to declare, implement, measure, and fulfill objectives.

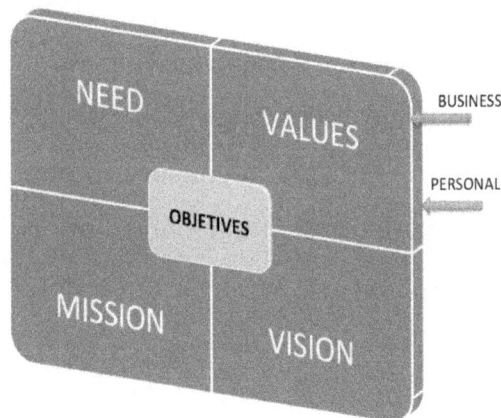

Goals are established objectives that must be achievable, measurable, and understandable. Above all, goals must have people who are responsible for them. We have encountered organizations that have very well-designed mission statements along with infallible measurement and monitoring methods, but which are weak in that the people responsible for the activities needed to meet objectives are not clearly identified.

This is where a common goal found throughout the organization, such as customer care, becomes a mystery distributed amongst everyone, without a leader or person responsible for the measurement or fulfillment of that goal.

When you set goals, it is because you have already defined where the organization is going. Therefore it is very important to know the mission and vision, because that is the basis from which you design activities, tasks and actions that allow you to achieve the objectives.

Goals should have the following elements:

1. Describe what is to be achieved in a clear, simple, and understandable way.
2. Set a goal for which the achievement of the objective can be measured.
3. Declare a term, period, or time for the accomplishment.
4. Establish a leader and people responsible for the objectives.
5. Set periods of evaluation and measurement of the objectives.
6. Perform monitoring with the established method or pattern of measurement.
7. Compare with previous measurements, and analyze behavior.
8. Create adjustments and methods for improving compliance.
9. Document all the steps above to create the records necessary to enable you to show the progress, compliance, and monitoring of your organization's system.

# Determine your Skills

| TALENTS | ABILITY/ DEXTERITY | KNOWLEDGE | ACTTITUDE | PASSION |
|---|---|---|---|---|
|  |  |  |  |  |
|  |  |  |  |  |
|  |  |  |  |  |
|  |  |  |  |  |
|  |  |  |  |  |
|  |  |  |  |  |
|  |  |  |  |  |
|  |  |  |  |  |
|  |  |  |  |  |
|  |  |  |  |  |
|  |  |  |  |  |
|  |  |  |  |  |
|  |  |  |  |  |
|  |  |  |  |  |
|  |  |  |  |  |
|  |  |  |  |  |
|  |  |  |  |  |
|  |  |  |  |  |
|  |  |  |  |  |
|  |  |  |  |  |
|  |  |  |  |  |
|  |  |  |  |  |

## CHAPTER 3 (Day 7)

## Develop Your Strategic Business Plan

Strategic planning allows you to combine all the information we developed in the previous chapter into an action plan to achieve your goals. This journey we have made through reading, analysis, and the completion of the forms is the basis for the construction of strategic planning. With an overview of the organization you can have good administration of each of the processes and resources. Also, it enables you to change your focus from the day-to-day activities performed within your organization and provides a global perception that directs you to where you should be going.

In order to create a good strategic plan, it is necessary for each of the board members of the organization to be present and to participate in an interactive way, knowing that this step takes time and dedication, but that the benefits obtained are of great help to the business.

It is important that each of the partners prepare the information independently and that afterwards, the documentation is discussed in joint work sessions.

This activity allows you to compare ideas and concepts that each member of the organization has about the business, just as in the previous chapter you were able to determine the vision, mission, and objectives of your organization.

In this part, it is recommended that each of the partners or decision-makers in the organization responds to the following questions:

**Questions for the members of the organization**

1. Who are we as an organization?
2. What capacity do we have?
3. What can we do?
4. What is the main problem at hand?
5. What are our major strengths and resources?
6. What is our priority now?

Once each member has described his or her views on the answers to these questions, they must come together and share this information to integrate it into a single document.

If at the time of the meeting there is a diversity of approaches, this is normal and beneficial because it allows everyone to express a vision of the organization and then to adjust their visions towards the same path.

This activity should be done with the attitude and willingness to learn that we should not reject differences, but value them as a source of new information, which allows us to nurture the variety of elements that a business may contain.

Many times people focus on defending a point of view because they want to be right, more so than because the specific issue is important to them. It is important to keep this principle in mind when doing this activity, and to maintain an adult attitude and stay focused on the benefit to the organization.

When people want to develop a business or already have one and want it to grow, the attitude should be to make decisions that benefit the business more than the personal and individual concerns of each member; this is one of the primary values that must be established. It is known that people have emotional burdens that might be the source of differences and discussions within an organization, but those emotions need not disappear; rather, they should be directed to generate benefits for the business.

## SWOT Development

The meaning of the initials SWOT is Strengths, Weaknesses, Opportunities, and Threats.

This technique is very old, but very easy to manage so that people can visualize in a practical way the strengths and/or weaknesses of the business, as well as the opportunities and threats in the environment.

It is recommended to use an external facilitator or consultant for the development of this technique, for several reasons listed below.

## Reasons to have a consultant

1. An independent person from outside the organization, preferably an experienced consultant, can objectively manage the points to be discussed without emotions that may influence the resulting information.

2. The members of the organization will feel free to comment without any pressure from having the meeting led by a business partner.

3. The external person has the skills of conflict management and negotiation, so that the group feels comfortable and proactive.

4. The consultant manages the SWOT tools well in order to take advantage of every evaluation aspect and can get the best out of the members of the organization.

5. The person has a fresh vision and is not biased towards developing a preferred aspect, since the person has no internal interests involved.

6. The person is someone with experience and professionalism who can handle the information objectively and with integrity.

## EXTERNAL FACTORS

In any organization there are internal and external factors that directly affect the functioning of a business. We begin by analyzing the external factors that can have an influence.

**Demographic:** This represents the structure and dynamics of populations, as well as their formation, maintenance, and disappearance. This demographic analysis allows us to observe the behavior of the population in order to understand how your business can meet the needs of local or non-local markets, using quantitative data on fecundity, mortality, immigration and emigration, etc.

In this section, you should know in which geographic area you wish to position your business so that you can get to know the scope and behavior, and be clear about the opportunities and threats for your business in the area where you want to develop.

**Economic:** Economic issues relate both to the area where the organization is as well as where the customers are. It is important to recognize what economic situation exists in the environment to be able to put a value on the product and/or service that the organization provides.

It is very important to keep in mind the economic situation where the business and the service or product you offer are located, and the market segment to which your service or product is directed. Recognizing the socioeconomic strata you are focused on and managing the potential customer's economic ability to acquire your service or product is an important contribution to the strategic planning of the organization.

This information is not only relevant for knowing the market but also for managing the costs of manpower, raw materials, and services associated with the production and presentation of your product or service. This analysis allows you to evaluate the supply chain to determine adjustments that can minimize cost and allow you to be more competitive in the market.

**Social:** This area is closely related to the combination of economic and demographic factors, as certain aspects of social behavior arise as the economy influences the behavior of a society. When this is combined with regulation, legal and systematic elements are created that influence the environment and can affect the behavior of society when it comes time to buy your organization's service or product.

This analysis of social behavior goes hand in hand with fashion, media, and society's tastes, and is also related to the cultural, racial, and stylistic groups towards which you will direct your service or product.

**Regulatory:** The regulatory aspect relates to how your business is impacted by government regulations that surround your industry, community, or zoning. Regulations include social policies that influence the conduct of society and may affect your customers, employees, suppliers and whether the activities of the business comply with such regulations. It is important to know current and pending future regulations that may change the way you do business.

**Cultural:** This refers to the behaviors, tastes, and habits of groups of persons or members of a community, region, or country. When we refer to culture in business, this means determining the beliefs, rules, and knowledge of the region where our services and products are going to be marketed, as well as the material they use, their technology, communication, and ways of handling situations in general.

It is important to know very well the culture of the area where we want to expand our business, because it must be done in such a way that rejection will not occur, making it more difficult to establish the business.

**Legal:** These are the regulations and other legal aspects that are related to your business and govern the market environment. The legal aspects are very important when you know what type of regulations affect the presentation of the service or product, how they affect taxes and penalties, the legal aspects of labor, distribution, storage, production, and raw material.

You must carefully examine the activities of your organization and how laws and regulations affect your business.

**Technological:** The evaluation of your organization's production processes and how technology is affecting the product or service you offer. Technological changes are accelerating, and engaging internal processes with the external reality of technological change is very important and can deeply affect and impact your organization.

For example, you can offer a service or product for which the means of distribution or production varies depending on how it integrates the technological reality that changes from day to day. You could be very successful or just disappear from the market according to how your company adapts or fails to adapt to these changes.

**Ecological:** This aspect refers to the way in which the product or service your organization provides affects the environment, both positively and negatively. This evaluation can open up new opportunities and prevent any legal aspects involving a penalty, as well as providing benefits for the development of ecological activities that care for the environment.

All these aspects of the environment should be analyzed in terms of opportunities and threats, and should be described in the form: **"Opportunities and Threats"**. When you complete each box with an external analysis of each element, you must also fill in the box indicating action, as this is where you deal with the facts involved in the opportunity or threat that your organization faces. It is important that you carefully develop every line of analysis, because this is how you will be able to think of the direct actions you must take in order to take advantage of the opportunity and minimize or prevent the threat.

## INTERNAL FACTORS

To analyze internal factors, it is necessary to keep in mind the type of organization and, in many cases; the areas described below may vary depending on your organization. In this analysis we will manage the **weaknesses and strengths** of each of the areas.

We are listing some areas that many organizations have in common, but remember that there may be some other specific areas depending on the type of organization you have.

**Organizational structure:** Here we must evaluate the strengths of your business in terms of having a descriptive chart that reflects the lines of command within the organization. However small it may be, it is important to be clear about the positions of the members and the various roles and responsibilities of each person. If nothing like this exists, it should be considered a weakness and the reason for it should be explained.

**Strategic Planning:** What we did in chapters two and three of this book are the activities necessary to establish strategic planning within the organization, so when you are developing this activity you can determine it as a strength; and the weakness could be the lack of strategies in the past and the failure to perform actions that may have been established.

**Human Resources:** This refers to the management of staff within the organization. It is the control of both administrative and professional staff in terms of qualifications, training, evaluation, promotion, development plans, etc.

You need to determine exactly how you are managing your own area of human resources; to analyze whether you have future plans for training; to recognize areas where there are internal weaknesses that affect the development of the human capital that is the backbone of any organization. Strength and weaknesses involving intellectual capital include what is known and what is unknown. What information is shared and what is kept secret by individuals, departments, and subject matter experts? Is information known, secure, and kept confidential? What does your company know compared with competition and is the value retained when and if employees leave?

**Marketing and Sales:** Any type of organization, whether manufacturing or service, must have a method to market itself and to sell. You need to have a plan, methods, and actions to sell what you produce. Examine whether you have any formal method established for marketing your products or services. Verify whether this method is effective and your sales increase with time. Establish which strengths and weaknesses you have in the area of marketing your business.

**Administration and Finance:** Refers to all the administrative activities of a business, including accounts receivable, accounts payable, bank costs, the entire administrative control, whether these things are done regularly, as well as accounting, tax returns, etc.

Whether you do these activities or outsource them to third parties, you should check that they are being done regularly and effectively.

**Maintenance & Facilities:** Every organization has an infrastructure where work is done, whether this is an office, equipment, computers, or vehicles. All elements of this infrastructure must be maintained and controlled, and must be effective so that you can meet the client's requirements.

When we speak of maintenance, we must consider regularity, monitoring, technical conditions, and updating of the equipment, accessories, and devices involved in business productivity.

**Technology and communications:** The aspects of technology and communications must be monitored and evaluated, because in today's world dominated by technology, these elements are now key to being effective in the areas of operations, administration, human resources, marketing and sales, etc. Technological aspects are always linked and must be analyzed carefully in terms of updates, operation, maintenance and effectiveness.

The internal analysis should be developed on Form **"Strengths and Weaknesses"**. On this form, as on the previous form, you should develop internal analysis to evaluate each item and the actions to be taken both to maintain and build on the strengths, and to improve the weaknesses

# STRATEGIC PLANNING

Once you have completed "**Opportunities and Threats and "Strengths and Weaknesses**", combine all the information on form "**Strategic Planning**". Here you should write the activity or action to be done along with the start date, completion date, and person responsible for the activity.

This activity will allow you to establish a plan in the short, medium, and long term, and to establish monthly monitoring in order to act and make adjustments as necessary while the actions are executed.

This plan must have monthly monitoring, and it is advisable to make the necessary comments in the "Remarks" column so that you have evidence of monitoring and know what adjustments have been made to the plan.

Annually, do a full review, again applying all forms to determine whether there are any new elements that have not been analyzed and that have arisen in the course of time.

The annual review is very important because in that way you can determine how the organization has evolved, and which adjustments have been necessary due to the constant changes occurring in the market and in society. This review must be done with all the staff who originally participated so that each of the members can explain how actions were taken and their effectiveness, and any new suggestions, plans, and monitoring to complete.

## Opportunities and Threats

| AREA | OPPORTUNITIES | THREATS | ACTIONS |
|------|---------------|---------|---------|
| DEMOGRAPHIC | | | |
| ECONOMIC | | | |
| SOCIAL | | | |
| POLITIC | | | |
| CULTURAL | | | |
| LEGAL | | | |
| TECHNOLOGICAL | | | |
| ECOLOGICAL | | | |

# Strengths and Weaknesses

| AREA | STRENGTHS | WEAKNESSES | ACTIONS |
|---|---|---|---|
| ORGANIZATIONAL STRUCTURE | | | |
| STRATEGIC PLANNING | | | |
| HUMAN RESOURCES | | | |
| MARKETING AND SALES | | | |
| ADMINISTRATION AND FINANCE | | | |
| MAINTENANCE & FACILITIES | | | |
| TECHNOLOGY AND COMMUNICATIONS | | | |

## Strategic Planning

| ACTIVITY | START | END | RESPONSIBLE |
|---|---|---|---|
|  |  |  |  |
|  |  |  |  |
|  |  |  |  |
|  |  |  |  |
|  |  |  |  |
|  |  |  |  |
|  |  |  |  |
|  |  |  |  |
|  |  |  |  |
|  |  |  |  |
|  |  |  |  |
|  |  |  |  |
|  |  |  |  |
|  |  |  |  |
|  |  |  |  |
|  |  |  |  |
|  |  |  |  |

## CHAPTER 4 (Day 15)

## Establish Business Partner Agreements

When you decide to start a business, whether with one or more partners, you must understand that establishing agreements is an extremely important step because that is where the commitment of each person as members of a company begins.

At times it seems that relations between partners can be compared to a romantic relationship and even a marriage, as the ties established are similar; and respect, commitment, and open communication must be paramount, among others.

Management agreements must be concluded in writing. Although some successful partnerships have been established with a verbal commitment, this is not always effective. There must be a lot of personal integrity, and we will not always find partners who handle their verbal agreements with a **code of honor**. Not only for a business deal, but also for legal, administrative, and financial agreements, you must be able to show evidence if a legal problem arises. Here we will help you to have open communication with your business partners and to successfully document an agreement that is beneficial to the business and to each of the parties.

Each member must understand the role he or she plays within the organization and fulfill it responsibly, so if you establish a company where the percentage of shares is the same for each partner, responsibilities should be mostly distributed according to the abilities, skills, knowledge, and resources that each person possesses. The partners should consider which skills, abilities, and expertise they are best suited for.  When you have completed this task and the previous exercises, you then need to meet with the members of the organization with a view to establishing their roles, so that agreements are easier to make.

Identifying personal and professional skills is vital in creating this **code of honor**, which will help your organization stay afloat.  Each of the points that we are dealing with in this 90-day plan is essential for your business to establish solid foundations and effectively grow so you can start collecting the fruits.

Now, since you are in the fifteenth day of your plan, you have documented the mission, the personal and business visions, and the goals; this means that you know who you are and what your organization does.  You know where you are going and where the organization is going.  Therefore, each partner must act according to a common vision of where they want to go.

The following principles should be read and understood by each business partner and openly discussed to achieve a win-win agreement. Do not close a deal if some people feel that it is taking advantage of someone or something, or that they are the victim of an agreement that is not beneficial.  We know it is not easy to reach an agreement in which all members are happy with the same scenario, but you must make every effort and maintain sufficient maturity to not carry emotional burdens that sooner or later can damage the relationship between the partners.

This agreement must be understood, documented, and approved by mutual agreement of the members of the organization. It should look like the code of honor that will give them the moral and emotional foundation to go ahead with trust, respect, order, and above all with the peace of mind of having all the cards on the table with no hidden agendas, and no fears among the partners.

## PRINCIPLES TO FOLLOW

**1. Communication:** Establish the sort of communication that members will maintain between themselves, with employees, with customers, with suppliers, with third parties, with institutions, etc.

Remember that poor communication can cause incalculable problems within an organization, either through insufficient or excess communication, miscommunication, or manipulated communication; in short, this factor plays a decisive role when starting an organization.

The agreement of how to handle communication must be clear and explicit about the use of methods such as telephone, mail, billboards, notes, chat, paper correspondence, meetings, digital correspondence, voice communication, etc.

You must establish the type of information that will travel through different formats, as well as who will be targeted. To facilitate this statement, it may be based on a model that is appended to the end of the chapter "Model Communications Management", where you can tailor the information at your convenience.

On the other hand, communication agreements have certain codes that are important to observe in order to achieve greater effectiveness in managing the quality of information, such as:

- Know the phone numbers of members and their call schedules.
- Establish rules of time and manner for answering phone calls, voice messages, text messages, e-mail, etc.
- Create a standard business format for sending internal and external correspondence, and for the contact details at the end of each e-mail or document.
- Manage information verification techniques. For example, if you send an instruction to a person by any means of communication, request the person's understanding and interpretation of the message in order to verify comprehension.
- Create written minutes of agreements made in various meetings, and disclose them.
- Establish agreements on the management of personal and professional problems between partners and members of the organization.
- Establish agreements on how to handle customer information.
- Determine what information will be handled electronically and what will not.
- Use clear and precise language and do not manipulate or distort information.
- Ensure that levels of authority remain understood when decisions are made.

If these parameters are well-described and defined in the agreement you design for the organization, you will have another tool for avoiding problems, and will thus be able to better manage any eventuality.

When there are problems in this area, as a result other areas within the organization are affected; poor communication can create personal problems between partners and between employees, may result in the loss of customers, and can lead to legal problems. So you see the importance of having not only an agreement about managing communication, but also about how each member of the organization will ensure compliance.

In experiences with some of our clients, the issue of communication may be managed well by one or two members or partners, and there may be one who does not handle it so well. In these cases, if agreements are documented, members can refer to them, and can remind the person that he or she is not complying. In this way it becomes a rule that is not imbued with personal emotion; it simply happens to be a rule that has been set by the organization, and that must be followed. Note the difference between speaking to a partner about an e-mail he has not answered, and he says he was unaware that he should answer all e-mails, and relying on an agreement while explaining that he must comply with what he has signed. In the first case, a personal and emotional problem may be generated among the partners because they may believe that it's a personal situation. In the second case, by relying on a document, emotions are lowered and the emotional weight is transferred to the document, not the person.

**2. Commitment:** The commitment among members of the business is an agreement based on the values of the partners who demonstrate a duty to themselves as shown in social, family, and personal areas. A committed person is one who meets his or her obligations, whether they are those agreed on with other people, or their family, personal, work, and study obligations.

A commitment can be an agreement between two people and does not necessarily have to be in writing. Thus, many partners can create verbal commitments that they must adhere to and demonstrate in the course of the business relationship.

The important thing about this agreement is that each party understands his or her responsibilities and obligations within the business; it should be written so that there is a standard to be referred to in the partnership agreement.

The commitment and obligations may be lists of activities, phrases, instructions, for the purpose of the partners reaching a set agreement so that responsibility and professionalism govern in the business that is being established. This list of commitments can be determined in a common document called the *partner agreement* which must be signed by each of the members, or they may develop a "letter of commitment" in which each person in a particular way signs his or her commitment to the organization.

This aspect of the partnership agreement is quite open and can be spread among the other points we are dealing with in this chapter. You can make commitments about responsibilities, communications, and confidentiality issues, among others. If there is an obligation that you want to establish and it is not found in the other points of the agreement, you can design a particular list and declare it in that section of the partnership agreement.

To give you some ideas, we will present some commitments that certain companies have established and that have become part of their success:
- Maintain the ethics of product image in the media.
- Pay employees without delay or arrears.
- Commit to the prevention of accidents and work-related illnesses.

- Hire persons who are competent for the positions they will fill.
- Respect for the rules and internal guidelines, from both partners and employees.
- Maintain open and transparent communication between the partners.

**3. Responsibilities:** You already have enough material to establish the responsibilities of each partner, since you know their skills, knowledge, and commitments. Now you must personally declare the responsibilities of each member of the business.

Responsibilities should be handled by mutual agreement. Each person establishes the roles to be fulfilled and shares them with other partners, so that there is balance within the organization. For if one partner is very good at public relations, contacting people, and sales, then this person should be responsible for the marketing area; while another who is good at managing, dealing with documents, and crunching numbers will be responsible for management. Both roles may be shared at some point, because the management person may sell well, but that will be his or her second option to support the sales of the business, which is the area for which the other person is responsible.

It is important to know that partners should be responsible for the activities in which they have more experience and knowledge; and they must ensure there is management, implementation and monitoring in these areas, for which they can get help from other members.

What should be defined is the distribution of roles and responsibilities of each partner, which must be declared regarding issues such as business areas that will be strategically managed, and small activities that are often seen as of little importance and so are not reported, but which could be a factor in future problems.

"Small activities" can refer to things like the management of banking activities, for example, or statements made to government entities, payments for office services, purchases of business cards, etc. These little things should be the responsibility of one of the partners if you start a small business and do not have staff.

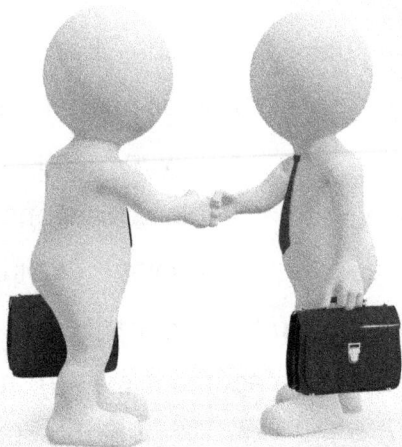

The statement of responsibilities of the partners goes hand in hand with the commitments. It is important that once the responsibilities are declared, you verify that these are in line with the commitments set out previously.

Creating a business while assuming each partner will play certain roles, without making a formal declaration, can generate serious conflicts ranging from loss of money, to the breakdown of the company. We have handled many cases in small and medium enterprises that began with the assumption of good faith and assumptions on the part of the members. This status works for some time, possibly up to several years. But when the company starts to grow or suffers from any change in the market, each partner begins to fight and defends his or her area of responsibility, assuming that someone was responsible for an activity because that person had been doing it, and meanwhile the other person feels he or she was working inappropriately hard. These kinds of emotions, conflicts, and feelings can damage business relationships as well as personal relationships, and create scars which then become very difficult to bear.

**4. Conflict of Interest:** Conflicts of interest are a very thin line that can often be overlooked and not observed; they may be real or imagined. Even if there is no conflict of interest, if someone thinks there is, this can cause problems; for this reason, it is very important to avoid the appearance of a conflict of interest, as well as actual conflict of interest. The perception that there is a conflict of interest can damage both the reputation of an individual and of a business.

One of the measures that can be taken to prevent conflicts of interest is to express verbally or in writing to the partners the sort of activities that could potentially generate a conflict of interest within your organization, whether in personal, financial, social, or political areas.

When establishing the commitments and responsibilities, you must make very clear the actions each partner should take to avoid conflicts of interest affecting the business.

We can detect a conflict of interest when an element comes into play that benefits a person independently and not the business or organization as such; it can also be seen in hidden aspirations of power that some of the partners have that may interfere with their established responsibilities.

For responsible management of these conflicts, we can use an arbitrator. This can be a consultant, an adviser, or a person outside the business who can play that role and help negotiate with, mediate among, and reconcile

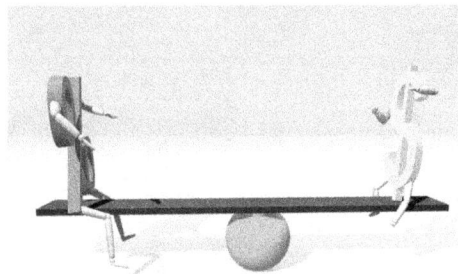

the parties involved in the conflict.

Another element that helps prevent conflicts of interest is to establish internal standards and procedures for the organization. Having established written standards makes it easier to determine whether or not a conflict exists.

It is recommended that these standards be declared in sentences such as those written in the section on commitments. List them in this section and establish the interests that are critical for the organization.

We will provide some examples to make it easier for you to write your own:

- Refrain from engaging in activities (personal, social, financial, or political) that can conflict with the loyalty, value judgments, or objectivity of the management of the organization.
- Immediately inform the partners when considering an activity that could be taken as a conflict of interest, and discuss the matter to arrive at a common agreement.
- Avoid making hidden agreements with suppliers, customers, or competitors without the approval of all of the members of the organization.
- Avoid developing, marketing, distributing, or doing any personal activity with a service or product that could be in competition with services or products generated by the organization.

**5. Remuneration:** Each partner has a percentage of shares in the organization, and based on that percentage, the company's profits should be distributed at the end of the time period or fiscal year as declared by the partners. In most cases when organizations are in their infancy, the partners do not take this benefit; rather, they reinvest it in the business. In other cases, there is no profit in the first year or two, and that should not be a concern if the basic costs are being covered and the partners' investment of time is being rewarded.

Here you must establish and clearly define the investment of time and money on the part of each partner, since there are venture capitalists or so-called investors, and industrial partners who contribute their work.

When an investor brings money, he or she need not contribute labor. Similarly, an industrial partner need not contribute money. There may also be a combined version where there is a contribution of both money and labor.

The theme of work and knowledge is a very delicate point when the business wishes to measure this type of contribution. The best practice is to estimate the time and effort invested by the industrial partner so that each of the parties understands from the beginning what the contributions have been.

Many companies start with the excitement of opening a new business and as they encounter the difficulties that every business has, they feel that the worker has tried harder than the one who provided the money; or on the contrary, the contributor of the funds feels the other is not working well, and that the money invested has been put at risk. For these situations, it is advisable to establish mutually agreed contributions and payments when profits are distributed.

It is important to clarify that operating costs are different from profit distribution; many small businesses do not control the operation, and when a sale is made they distribute the profits between the partners without estimating the commission and the effort of the partner who got the client or who performed the service. It is important to know the management and administration costs so that this distribution will be equitable and partners will feel they are giving a balanced effort when they put in their time and money.

When you start a business and this creates monthly profits but the partners do not receive money every month, this may cause dissatisfaction and lack of motivation. That is why you must understand what work activities are done daily in the business, and know how to manage the finances in case of exclusive investment.

Every business is different in the way it manages remuneration, and it is difficult to provide a generic recommendation, but we can offer the following considerations:

- State the type of partner (capitalist, industrial, capitalist-industrial).
- In the case of industrial partners, determine the time invested when managing the operating costs of the organization.
- Declare arrangements for sharing profits at a frequency that benefits both the partners and the company.
- Determine whether compensation will be 100% of profits, or what percentage of profits will be reinvested in the business.
- Partners must set the value of money and of shares for the profit distribution process.

**6. Confidentiality:** this means the confidentiality of information, data, material, products, etc. that are deemed to be for the exclusive use of members of the organization, and cannot be disclosed, shared, or made accessible to third parties or to persons who have not been authorized by the organization.

The information can be in different kinds of media, whether print, digital, video, sound, or any other kind.

We can give some examples of confidential information:

- The organization's internal operations, such as recipes, formulas, processes, procedures, etc.
- The personal information of employees, customers, and suppliers.
- Software, data, licenses.
- Costs and handling of raw materials, services.
- Wages and salaries, compensation.
- Partner remuneration.

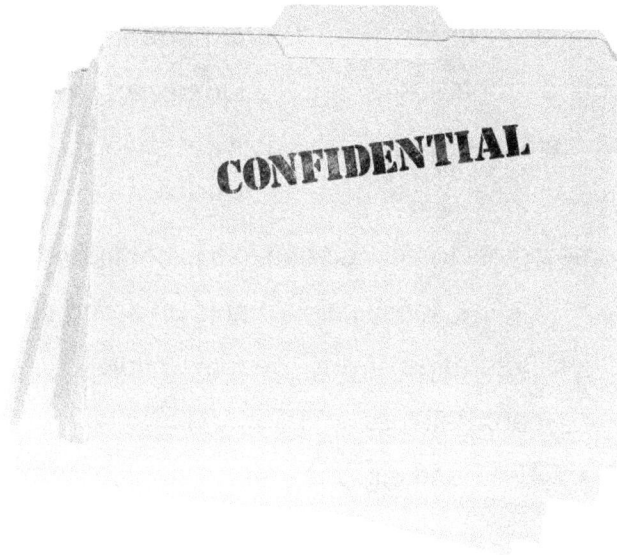

When you want to have confidentiality agreements, you can have separate letters of confidentiality for workers and partners. If there is a consultant, auditor, or external service company working within the organization, it is advisable that they sign such an agreement or letter, so that you can protect your organization. In the partners' case, this agreement can be in a general document that deals with all the points found in this chapter.

It is important to establish and classify which information will be handled as confidential, as this way you will be better able to set the guidelines.

These confidentiality agreements must be reviewed frequently, perhaps every six months, in order to ensure important areas are covered and areas that do not require control are not included, as well to update the agreements due to technological, social, and political changes.

Some points to be included in the confidentiality agreement are:

- Define specifically what is declared confidential.
- Determine if the people involved in the agreement are individuals or corporations.
- The handling of exceptions, although in some cases this may not apply to confidentiality.
- What kind of legal or judicial sanctions are involved, as well as sanctions within the organization.
- Determine the time limits of the sanctions or the expiry date of the confidentiality agreement.
- Cover areas, processes, information, time, and people.

Signature

## DEFINING THE AGREEMENT

To conclude this chapter, you can take the elements that you consider important and applicable to your organization from each principle in order to develop a single document containing all of the agreements. Each partner will sign, and there will be a copy for the partner and one for the organization's records. You can also develop a separate document for each principle and tailor it to each partner and/or member of the organization, assuming each will be signed and received by the organization and partners.

These agreements or contracts between partners are vital to a foundation of commitment and responsibility that creates an environment of transparency in the organization. Remember the old saying that he who does not should not be afraid; the more information that is openly recorded, the better the relationship between the partners will be.

## CHAPTER 5 (Day 17)

## Establish Internal Competencies and Roles

Whether your company is big, medium, or small, it is necessary to establish the responsibilities of each person in the organization. These responsibilities must be associated with the competencies required by each worker to fulfill his position. We have found that some companies have grown rapidly and are not prepared for changes. They show weaknesses in that some positions are designed according to the competence of the person who is currently in the position and not as they should be, where the position has been established to provide the competencies the organization requires, so it can be exercised regardless of who is currently in that position. In short, the position has been designed according to the person who is in it and not according to what the company really needs. When this person leaves, the organization is not really clear what the powers of the office should be, and this creates disorder which requires the adjustment and movement of many pieces in order to correct it.

So even if your organization is very small, it is recommended that you establish the roles of each member, as well as the structure of a functional flow chart, creating lines of control that are grouped by functional areas and that permit the flow of information and the best performance of the organization.

In this chapter, we will help you determine the skills required in the basic positions of your organization, as well as to define the skills required of the personnel you already have. With this information you can capture on a map or functional flow chart how the functions relate to the positions within your organization.

We will provide practical and easy-to-use tools so that you can go to work as a Human Resources Specialist with the vision of an innovative entrepreneur.

## STEP 1

Make a list of activities that your company does, such as purchasing, processing, storage, sale, distribution, service provision. Create an entire detailed list of activities in any order. As you remember them, list them on the paper.

## STEP 2

Once you have the list of activities, organize them by groups depending on who does them. Put the activity in one column, and in another column write the name of the person responsible. In this way, you can group them by person and area.

## STEP 3

With the activities organized by responsibility, add one more column where you put the name of the position that you believe should be responsible for that group of related activities. In this step you connect the positions with their activities.

## STEP 4

With the support of the **Position Description Form**, you can fill out every box with the information requested, and you will use it in this way for each position you have in the organization, as well as the positions that you require. An example of a position description is attached for guidance.

## STEP 5

When you have finished filling out the form above, you should compare the section "Position Requirements and Knowledge, Abilities and Skills" with the person who is currently in the position. That way you can find the gap between what that person has and what he or she needs to develop to execute the position with the best possible skill. In this case, fill out and use the **Competency Screening Form**.

## STEP 6

In filling out the **Competency Screening Form**, determine the priorities that require immediate action and those that can wait. In this way, you will know whether you are able to invest the time and money required to cover the gap that may be causing your organization to lose power.

## STEP 7

With the above steps you can start to create the flow chart of your business, as guided by the "Coordination and Communication" section of the **Position Description Form**. There, you will be able to assemble the pieces to design the flow chart of the organization.

**Guidelines for the design of a flow chart**

For the design of the flow chart, it is important to understand that the first design will never be the final one, and that this is normal. In the development of flow charts there may be several versions that are upgraded and adjusted over time. If you are following the steps in this book, you can take a couple of hours and explore the Internet for information about how to design a flow chart, and that will give you more knowledge on the subject. Nevertheless, we offer some simple tips to complete this model of your organization that will help you to continue the sequence of activities planned for the following days.

- Define what type of organizational structure you want to design, whether it is structured on the basis of the functions or job descriptions that have been developed, according to products so that people's positions are organized by the type of product or service provided, or by customer or region.

- Decide the type of chart or form of presentation that you want, whether drawn in a vertical or horizontal way, or in blocks. Very simple tools are found in some presentation management software, in which model flow charts have been pre-designed.

- Establish the position levels to be developed; fewer levels are best for easy organizational management and minimizing hierarchies.

- Join the positions with connecting lines according to hierarchy and management authority, as the case may be, for example: linear boss-subordinate relationships, advisory relationships, relationships of specialized control, external relations, etc.

- Fill the boxes with the names of the positions and the name of each person occupying each position, as well as those cases where there is nobody covering some positions, which you must declare as "vacant".

- Set the date and version of the flow chart to control its update every time you need to make a change.

**Example of a Functional Organization**

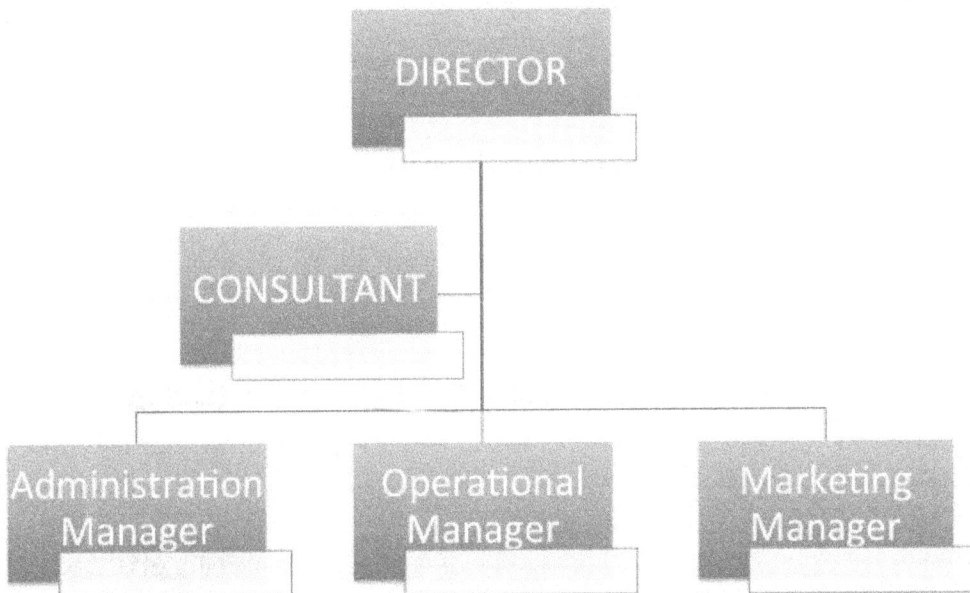

```
                        ┌──────────────┐
                        │   DIRECTOR   │
                        │  ┌────────┐  │
                        └──┴────────┴──┘
                               │
        ┌──────────────┐       │
        │  CONSULTANT  │───────┤
        │  ┌────────┐  │       │
        └──┴────────┴──┘       │
                               │
   ┌───────────────┬───────────┴───────────┬───────────────┐
┌──────────────┐    ┌──────────────┐    ┌──────────────┐
│Administration│    │  Operational │    │   Marketing  │
│   Manager    │    │    Manager   │    │    Manager   │
│ ┌─────────┐  │    │ ┌─────────┐  │    │ ┌─────────┐  │
└─┴─────────┴──┘    └─┴─────────┴──┘    └─┴─────────┴──┘
```

## Example:  Position Description

| Position title: | Line of dependency: |
|---|---|
| Office Manager | Administration Management |

| Purpose of the position: | Position Requirements |
|---|---|
| Coordinate, direct and control the business processes of the organization, applying established rules and procedures, in order to support the Operations Manager in organizing various activities to ensure effective service delivery. | **Education:**<br><br>Intermediate-level Technician<br><br>**Experience:**<br>2 years |

| Functions: | Knowledge,  Abilities, Skills. |
|---|---|
| 1.  Plan and follow up on the commercial, tax, and legal obligations of the business.<br>2.  Supervise the Administration area.<br>3.  Check and run the verification processes for accounts payable, accounts receivable, purchasing, payroll, HR, and other activities directly related to the administrative process.<br>4.  Coordinate, direct, and control staff pay.<br>5.  Put expense tracking into effect.<br>6.  Participate in the taking of physical inventory, both assets and inputs.<br>7.  Coordinate and control the hiring and leaving of personnel, and other labor-related duties.<br>8.  Determine the preparation of customer invoices together with the Operations Manager. | **Knowledge:**<br>➢ Bilingual (English-Spanish)<br>➢ Records management<br>➢ Office and accounting technology<br>➢ Appropriate use of the telephone<br>➢ Management and organization of the agenda<br>➢ Correspondence drafting |

| | |
|---|---|
| 9. Develop, coordinate, and control staff contracts. | ➤ Effective communication. |
| 10. Coordinate and track customers' accounts receivable and maintain a weekly updated report for presentation at meetings. | |
| 11. Input all daily transactions into the accounting system and generate the reports established in internal processes and procedures. | **Abilities:**<br><br>➤ Leadership<br>➤ Tact and prudence for managing diverse situations |
| 12. Issue a monthly general report of all administrative transactions. | |
| 13. Provide customer service either by phone or in person, managing any administrative transaction, complaint, or claim. | ➤ Courtesy, kindness, respect |
| 14. Under the supervision of the Operations Manager, maintain constant communication with the Operations Assistant to exchange information regarding production. | **Skills:**<br><br>➤ Computer management |
| 15. Establish improvements to optimize processes. | ➤ Creativity and innovation |
| 16. Fulfill any other functions, duties, and responsibilities arising from or related to the position, as required by the company and its current and future customers. | ➤ Teamwork<br>➤ Sense of belonging to the organization |

| COORDINATION AND COMMUNICATION | |
|---|---|
| **Relationships** | **With whom?** |
| **External** | Clients, service providers |
| **Internal** | The position maintains direct communication with the Administration Manager, Operations Manager and Assistant Operations |
| **Position Supervisor:** | Administration Manager |
| **Supervisory Responsibilities:** | None |

## ENVIRONMENT AND WORK RISKS

**Work Environment:** The office is located in a closed room in a cold environment, generally agreeable.

**Risk:** The position is exposed to different types of risks as set forth in the position risk notice.

**Effort:** The position requires the physical exertion of constant sitting and standing, and requires an average degree of manual and visual precision

# Position Description

| Position title: | Line of dependency: |
|---|---|

| Purpose of the position: | Position Requirements |
|---|---|
| | **Education:**<br><br>**Experience:** |

| Functions: | Knowledge, Abilities, Skills. |
|---|---|
| | **Knowledge:**<br><br>**Abilities:**<br><br>**Skills:** |

90 Day Challenge

| COORDINATION AND COMMUNICATION | |
|---|---|
| Relationships | With whom? |
| External | |
| Internal | |
| Position Supervisor: | |
| Supervisory Responsibilities: | |

| ENVIRONMENT AND WORK RISKS |
|---|
| Work Environment:<br><br>Risk:<br><br>Effort: |

## COMPETENCY SCREENING

| Position Title | Need Training | Priority | Name of Activity |
|---|---|---|---|
| | | | |
| | | | |
| | | | |
| | | | |
| | | | |
| | | | |
| | | | |
| | | | |
| | | | |
| | | | |
| | | | |
| | | | |

Training for the position can be done internal or externally, through position exchange, visiting other companies, induction, buying books, online training, working with another person, etc.

# CHAPTER 6 (Day 22)

## Key Business Processes and Procedures

For both administrative and operating performance, it is necessary to establish internal procedures that give every person in the organization a guideline to follow. In this phase of your plan, you first need to make a list of possible basic processes that your organization must have.

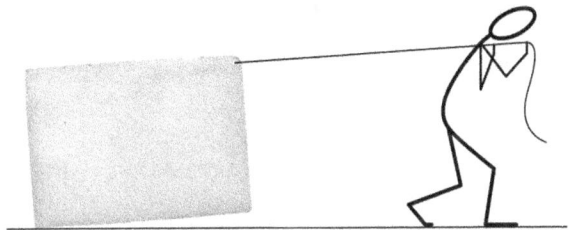

Later we will give you a standard list of certain fundamental processes, but there are specific processes that depend on the type of organization you have, and they should be developed by an internal organization team or by a consultant.

These processes should be classified into three groups: strategic, operational, and support processes. This classification will give you a basis for measuring the processes we will explain in the next chapter.

A process can have several associated procedures that support its internal activities. For example, within the purchasing process you can have the procedures for finding suppliers, requests for proposal, receipt of materials, etc. Each procedure has a breakdown of the activities carried out by leaders, resources, and places. In this way, everyone knows the steps to follow and you will have better control of your organization without having to be 100% involved in every area.

What happens in some organizations that do not have this vision of organizing processes and procedures is that they may start very small, but as they grow in an accelerated manner, the business owners have two options: one is to become slaves to the business, which will mean that every day they will have less time to handle the volume of activities, as business goes well but quality of life decreases. The other option is to continue at the same pace as in the beginning or perhaps more slowly, believing that the company is growing and they can let their guard down; but if this growth is not organized it can be reversed quickly, and with bigger problems.

We have had clients who stayed in the comfort zone, thinking that the business was growing and needed no control, because the numbers in the bank made it appear to be working very well. But remember, the fact that money is coming into the company does not mean all is well. These customers continued to work in the same way as at the beginning of the business, but now in a larger organization with more customers, more services, and more products. In this way bigger problems started, which they were not able to handle. Unfortunately productive enterprises had losses, in some cases right up to the closure of the business.

With these experiences of companies that were once successful, we want to show you the importance of establishing processes and procedures so that you can measure the performance of your organization. Sometimes business owners do not perceive this situation because it presents itself slowly over the years, and they believe it is a temporary situation and external to them. That is why it is important to insist on control over your organization so that you do not go through these situations and have to close your business or try to keep it at a loss. Remember that what is not measured cannot be improved.

## Strategic Processes

- Strategic planning
- Financial management
- Marketing
- Research and development

## Operational Processes

- Purchasing
- Sales
- Warehouse
- Distribution
- Billing and collection
- Customer Service

## Support Processes

- Human Resources
- Computing
- Administration
- Accounting
- Maintenance
- Customer service
- Internal security

You can guide yourself with this list and add more processes or remove some of them, or change the places of some of them. That is to say, a strategic process can be in the operational area or an operational process can be put in the support area. All this depends on the type of organization. For example, for a service company that does not make many purchases except simple office supplies, the purchase process becomes a support process and not an operational process.

When the processes are defined, you must develop procedures that support each one of them. In this chapter, we offer some examples with job templates in order for you to understand the structure of the procedures and their scope.

| Billing procedure | Responsible |
|---|---|
| 1. Receive e-mail information from Sales specifying the reason and amount for billing the client. | 1. Sales Assistant |
| 2. Verify that the client to be billed is registered in the administrative system. If not registered, create a file for the client including fiscal information. | 2. Billing Analyst |
| 3. Enter the invoice to be issued into the administrative system according to the parameters received in the e-mail. | 3. Billing Analyst |
| 4. Check that the information of the client to be billed has been correctly input, as well as the description and amount. If there is any error, make the corresponding adjustments; otherwise, continue with the procedure. | 4. Billing Analyst |
| 5. Print the invoice, and check that it printed correctly. If there is any error, cancel the invoice; otherwise, continue with the procedure. | 5. Billing Analyst |
| 6. Remove the invoice and distribute it. | 6. Billing Analyst |
| 7. Write the "Acknowledgement of Receipt", print two copies, sign and seal them. | 7. Billing Analyst |
| 8. Put the invoice and the "Acknowledgement of Receipt" together and send them to the client. | 8. Billing Analyst |
| 9. Receive the "Acknowledgement of Receipt" that has been signed and sealed by the client, and file it in the client folder to keep track. | 9. Billing Analyst |

| Vendor payment procedure | Responsible |
|---|---|
| 1. Receive from Purchase Management the supplier's "Purchase and/or Service Order" and "Invoice". | 1. Purchasing Analyst |
| 2. Enter the invoice(s) received into the administrative system, along with applicable standard withholdings. | 2. Accounts Analyst |
| 3. Generate the standard withholdings through the system and attach them to the original invoice. | 3. Accounts Analyst |
| 4. File the "Purchase and/or Service Order", the "Invoice", and the "Proof of Withholding". | 4. Accounts Analyst |
| 5. Generate the "Payment Schedule List" previously authorized by the Administration Manager. | 5. Accounts Analyst |
| 6. Send the list of payments to the Administration Manager to proceed with mass payments to suppliers as authorized by the Treasurer. | 6. Accounts Analyst |
| 7. Receive authorization from the Treasurer to make mass payments to various suppliers. | 7. Administration Manager |
| 8. Enter the banking system with registered credentials and password, and perform the corresponding transfer. | 8. Administration Manager |
| 9. Print the proof of transfer and forward it to the Treasurer together with payment for reconciliation. | 9. Administration Manager |
| 10. Reconcile the payment in the administrative system and return it to the Accounts Payable Analyst for his or her records. | 10. Treasurer |
| 11. Have the proof of transfer and other documents sent to the Treasurer, attach the payment record to the supplier's request for payment, and file it in the company's records. | 11. Accounts Analyst |

| Bank reconciliation procedure | Responsible |
|---|---|
| 1. Ask the Administration Manager to generate the business's bank statements. | 1. Assistant Admin Mgr |
| 2. Generate the bank statements and send them to the Assistant Administration Manager. | 2. Assistant Admin Mgr |
| 3. Receive the statements and ask the Accounts Receivable and Accounts Payable Analysts for records of payments and collections made during the months. | 3. Assistant Admin Mgr |
| 4. Enter the information into the administrative system, using registered credentials and password. | 4. Assistant Admin Mgr |
| 5. Verify that all cash receipts and payments are entered into the system. If they are not entered, notify whoever is responsible for the entry; otherwise, continue with the procedure. | 5. Assistant Admin Mgr |
| 6. Verify that all cash receipts and payments are reflected in the bank statement. | 6. Assistant Admin Mgr |
| 7. Print the "Bank Reconciliation" and "Summary of Reconciliation" reports once the balances are equal. | 7. Assistant Admin Mgr |

| Procedure for application for a contribution analysis | Responsible |
|---|---|
| 1. Consult the registry of suppliers who can satisfy the requisition. | 1. Purchasing Analyst |
| 2. Develop a "Request for Quote" for each selected supplier, and send it by fax or e-mail. | 2. Purchasing Analyst |
| 3. Receive the quotes and record the information in the "Analysis of Quote" form. | 3. Purchasing Analyst |
| 4. Analyze the quotes according to price, lead-time, quality, guarantees for the product or service, delivery terms, transport, among other factors. | 4. Purchasing Analyst |
| 5. Select the supplier that offers the best deal according to the evaluated conditions; print the "Analysis of Quote" and attach it to the purchase record. | 5. Purchasing Analyst |
| 6. Send the purchase file to the Purchasing Manager for review and approval. | 6. Purchasing Analyst |
| 7. Receive the purchase file. If it is approved, issue the "Purchase and/or Service Order"; otherwise, end the procedure. | 7. Purchasing Analyst |

| Purchasing procedure | Responsible |
|---|---|
| 1. Receive the approved purchase process, to give continuity to the procedure. | 1. Purchasing Analyst |
| 2. Develop a "Purchase and/or Service Order" on behalf of the successful supplier. | 2. Purchasing Analyst |
| 3. Verify that vendor data and the description of the purchase and/or service are correct. | 3. Purchasing Analyst |
| 4. Print the "Purchase and/or Service Order", attach it to the purchase file, and send it to the Purchasing Manager for approval by signature. | 4. Purchasing Analyst |
| 5. Receive the purchase file, verify that the "Purchase and/or Service Order" is correctly written, and signed and sealed in approval. Otherwise, return it for corrections. | 5. Purchasing Analyst |
| 6. Receive the purchase file and send the "Purchase and/or Service Order" to the supplier. | 6. Purchasing Analyst |
| 7. Request the supplier's invoice upon receipt of the good or service, and activate the "Request for Payment" procedure. | 7. Purchasing Analyst |

## CHAPTER 7 (Day 30)

## Process Maps and Comprehensive View of the Business

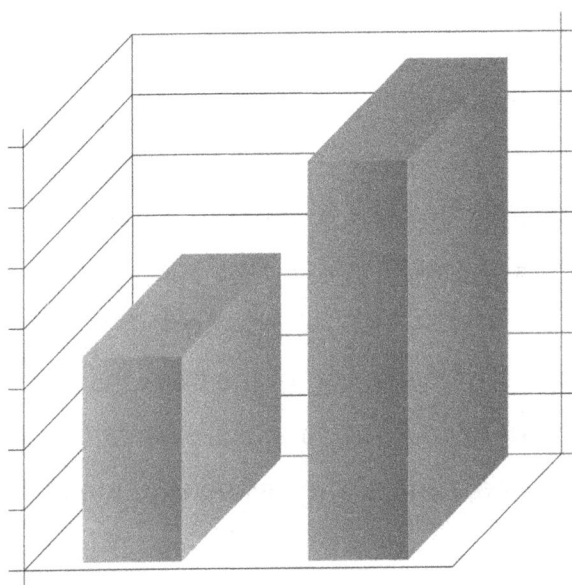

A desired result is achieved more efficiently when activities and resources are managed under a process approach, which should be presented as a system that is connected and is easy to identify, understand, and manage. One way to introduce this concept to organizations is by using a process map, which should show the interrelationships between processes and how these are combined with resources to achieve effectiveness and efficiency in achieving the objectives of the organization. This map should identify the processes the organization requires, in order to determine the process sequence and interrelationship that will allow creation of the service and/or product the organization produces.

A valuable element in the design of process maps is to determine their input and output elements and how they relate in order to optimize the resources are managed during the production process of the organization.

Some of the benefits of a well-designed process map are:

- Eliminate errors and waste that may affect resources such as materials, money, time, and products.

- Minimize delays in the processes and activities of the organization.
- Maximize use of the organization's assets such as equipment, money, and materials.
- Facilitate the use of resources and processes.
- Adaptability to changing needs in the use of processes.
- Provide competitive advantages to the organization.
- Reduce overstaffing.
- Easy method for measuring organizational management.

When these process maps are designed, they are like a general picture of the organization. It is a complete vision where a single image can show how the organization is functioning and thus give a better idea of how to improve the product or service provided. As mentioned at the beginning of the book, have the organizational plan in order so that it is easier to improve, to analyze situations, to make decisions, to adapt to any changes, and to continuously measure organizational behavior.

Steps in designing the process map:

**STEP 1:** Take the list of processes you made in the previous chapter where they were classified as strategic, operational, and support processes.

Strategic processes are those that support the management and leadership of the organization. They are the processes which by their nature should give the organization strategic direction for improvement and decision-making that generally affects all the other processes of the organization.

Operational processes are responsible for the daily management of the activities that are vital to the company; these processes are mainly those that affect the customer, service management, or production.

Support processes are those that support strategic and operational activities. They ensure the maintenance and smooth running of the operation of the organization. They are not the core processes of production, but they support its operation.

**STEP 2:** Write the processes in the process boxes as illustrated in the example at the end of this chapter, and begin placing the boxes in the corresponding areas.

**STEP 3:** Once you have the process boxes in each section, begin placing the connecting lines, which link information between one process box and another. This step must be performed very carefully as there may be relationships between one process and several others, as well as between several processes and one.

**STEP 4:** Determine the inputs and outputs of your process map. Double-check each box and the interactions established. This way, you verify and confirm that no processes were left out.

# STRATEGIC PROCESSES

| STRATEGIC PLAN | QUALITY | FINANCE |

# OPERATIONAL PROCESSES

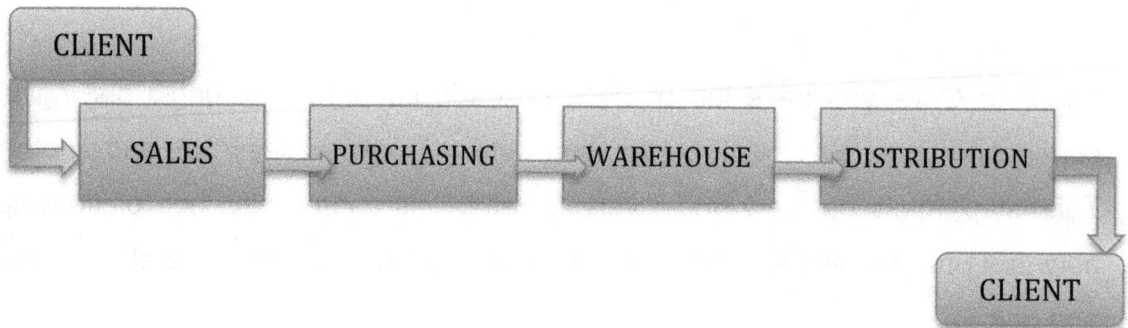

CLIENT

SALES → PURCHASING → WAREHOUSE → DISTRIBUTION

CLIENT

# SUPPORT PROCESSES

| MAINTENANCE | TECHNOLOGY | HUMAN RESOURCE |

**PROCESS MAP EXAMPLE**

90 Day Challenge

# PROCESS MAP

## STRATEGIC PROCESSES

## OPERATIONAL PROCESSES

## SUPPORT PROCESSES

## Management indicators

The power of measuring process management goes hand-in-hand with the establishment of performance indicators; these allow you to demonstrate in numbers the success or failure of the organization. The indicators provide insight into the performance of a process, activity or system.

An indicator should be:

- Objective; stated simply, without elements that allow assumptions or presumptions.
- Measurable; it must establish a quantitative value as a measurement standard and goal to achieve.
- Verifiable; the design of the indicator should be allowed to go to the source of the data and be able to verify each element that affects it.
- Valuable; it must add value to the decision-making process, and not be a burden but an element of support for the senior management of the organization.
- Communicated and published; it must be in a format easily disclosed within the organization.

## Types of indicators:

1. Operational or tactical indicators
2. Strategic or management indicators
3. Regulatory or outcome indicators

## 1. OPERATIONAL OR TACTICAL INDICATORS

Operational indicators are designed to monitor daily or weekly activities. They point to the operational area of the process map. Those responsible for keeping these indicators are managers with more operational responsibility and who are lower in the organization's hierarchy. Records of this type of indicator should be made daily or weekly. We recommend the use of automated spreadsheets to facilitate control of these records.

When presenting this type of indicator we recommend point graphs or pie charts, where you can observe its behavior in the short term, hourly, daily, or weekly. The person providing this indicator should not take more than fifteen minutes to give you the daily update.

## 2. STRATEGIC OR MANAGEMENT INDICATORS

Strategic indicators control the management of middle and top positions in the organization. They measure the strategic-level management of the organization with the aim of presenting the behavior of the processes on a monthly or quarterly basis. When these indicators are analyzed and action is taken, the results will be reflected in the next 90 days. This indicator takes information from the operational indicators. It can be represented as a bar graph, area chart, or line graph.

## 3. REGULATORY OR OUTCOME INDICATORS

These are created for the top management of the organization; they are part of the data that comes from the strategic or management indicators, and are aimed at monitoring compliance with the objectives of the organization as well as its mission and vision. They generally are dealt with quarterly, semi-annually or annually. They must be managed with much analysis and great detail, since they generate decision-making that impacts the entire organization. The results of these indicators allow evaluation of long-term actions, which must be adjusted and modified to fit the overall vision of the organization. Usually the results taken from these indicators can be seen after one year.

## METHODOLOGY

The method of preparing management indicators consists of identifying processes and their location, and then understanding what processes will be evaluated and controlled. Remember it is not necessary for all processes to be controlled. To start, you can select the most important processes, those that impact the productivity of the organization and those that result in delays, complaints, and claims for your organization. Later, when you are improving some areas, you can move on to others. Do not try to cover an entire organization. Go little by little, and in this way you can move forward safely.

It is recommended that once you have selected the appropriate processes for evaluation, you follow the next steps that we will explain:

**Step 1:** Make a list of the processes selected to be measured through management indicators.

**Step 2:** Use the form "Indicator Matrix" and begin filling the boxes with the information for each process as follows:

**PROCESS/TYPE:** In the first box, write the names of the process and area to be evaluated as well as the type of process, whether strategic, operational, or support.

**INPUT/OUTPUT:** Indicate which input and output information is involved in the process; i.e., what input data is required for the process to work, and what output it will generate.

**EXPECTATIONS:** This involves what the internal or external customer that generates the process expects to receive; how the customer wants the output of information generated by the process to be evaluated. Example: shipments delivered on time, satisfied customers, timely payment to suppliers, etc.

**INDICATOR NAME:** This is the name you will give to the indicator you are designing. For example: Customer satisfaction, Complaints response times, Control of rejections, etc.

**INDICATOR:** The description of the formula that will calculate the data generated by the process to be measured, for example: Production compliance = (days late/days scheduled) x 100.

**QUANTIFIER/FREQUENCY:** In "quantifier" you will write whether the unit of measurement that will express its indicator will be in days, percentage, quantity, etc. The frequency consists in determining how often you will make the measurement, whether daily, weekly, monthly, quarterly, etc.

**GOAL:** Refers to the objective to be achieved. You will determine the goal you want to achieve with the indicator that controls it. It is recommended that the target be written down after at least about three indicator measurements have been taken, in order to understand the behavior and select a goal that is not too easy, but not too difficult to achieve. For example: if you establish a control percentage of approved products and the behavior indicates it is at 75%, it is advisable to set a target of 85% in order to see if you can reach the indicator in a period of about a year, and when it happens, update the target again to 95 or 100%.

**RESPONSIBLE PERSON:** You must write the name of the person who will do the work and control the presentation of the indicator. It might be the same person or two different people, but the important thing is that responsibility is identified for each indicator that is established.

**Step 3:** Once you have all the indicators set, perform the distribution of responsibilities to each person and highlight the fulfillment of the frequency of measurement.

**Step 4:** Each area that manages the indicator should take the data and present it in the most appropriate format, whether in graphs, charts, or reports that permit objective analysis.

**Step 5:** Have weekly or monthly meetings where each person presents the indicator; that way you will have better control of the organization. Make comments and document them at each meeting to serve as evidence of the behavior of the indicator, and the effectiveness or lack thereof of the actions taken.

| TYPE OF PROCESS | INPUT/ OUTPUT | EXPECTATIONS | INDICATOR NAME | INDICATOR (FORMULA) | QUANTIFIER/ FREQUENCY | GOAL | RESPONSIBLE |
|---|---|---|---|---|---|---|---|
| | | | | | | | |
| | | | | | | | |
| | | | | | | | |
| | | | | | | | |
| | | | | | | | |
| | | | | | | | |

**MANAGEMENT INDICATORS**

CHAPTER 8 (Day 40)

## Design Your Business Marketing

The accelerated pace of technology requires that we develop skills to make inroads into a changing society, where markets must move very quickly and in the right direction.  In global trade, you must adapt your product or service to various sectors, groups, or markets.  However, these different groups see you and your organization as a single image under a digital interface -- your website - which can be visited worldwide. You must be able to manage this digital portal intelligently, because the dream of bringing in millions of customers via global access to your company can become a sad reality where your website has few or no visitors, let alone sales.

That feeling of believing that we could be visited by millions and millions of people, and that most of those people could be our customers, is an exciting sensation that can either finish with a happy ending, or turn into a worse nightmare than we ever imagined.

As entrepreneurs, we must have vision and enthusiasm to act quickly but with patience, and with a strategic and innovative focus that helps us move forward without wasting resources.  It is amazing how human beings act in times of scarcity and of plenty.  In times of scarcity, we act shrewdly to conserve resources; in times of abundance, we grow slow and confident that things will stay the way they are. The same thing happens when we enter technological society. It provides so many data resources, information, and access methods that we start feeling too secure, and we submerge ourselves in all this data and access without getting effective results.

We are now short of time in an environment where information and opportunities are abundant. It is important to discover the new skills that we must develop to survive.

**Advertising**

We attended a business meeting at the Chamber of Commerce. Most participants were owners of small and medium-sized businesses. The topic under discussion was advertising and marketing. This question arose: "What is the most effective way to get good publicity?" That gave rise to a discussion, and these comments were heard:

- "People do not pay attention to newspapers or radio."
- "I invested money in a website and paid for a number of social media memberships, and I have seen no results."
- "I have a contract with an advertising and marketing company that sends monthly bills, but I don't see the number of customers in my business growing."

These were the statements of some of the disgruntled business owners we met. It was a stampede of negativity, one right after the other. There seemed to be no escape. It was like a virus that spread in the meeting room, and it was as if no antidote could cure the disease. The speakers identified others who were responsible and could be blamed, such as the economy, the government, society, and the country.

## The Vaccine for the Virus

When they have good print or radio advertising, or even a good ad on a billboard, many business owners think they have paid the necessary marketing costs.

A customer may arrive and enter your business; but if your customers do not return, it shows that advertising, no matter how cost-effective and striking, only inspires the first visit of a client. In many cases the client may not return, because there is no need, or because the client is unhappy. The second reason will cause greater losses because a bad review of a business multiplies quickly and exponentially, especially today with the use of technology and social networking. This will make it very difficult to get back an unhappy customer, or to attract potential future customers.

When was the last time you saw a repeat customer in your business? When was the last time a customer recommended your business to a friend?

### Advertising by Word of Mouth

One of the most effective forms of advertising is word of mouth. Your business must create such a unique and profound experience that your client cannot resist telling a friend. If your company does not respond with intensity to its target market, and does not make people feel they must tell others about your business, you are wasting your time on marketing and advertising, and must drastically change your business vision.

The business owners who made the negative comments at the Chamber of Commerce event suffered losses because they relied solely on advertising to attract customers. They did not believe in, or did not know about, word-of-mouth advertising. They thought advertising could make up for what was missing in their businesses.

If you manage to convince a person to enter your business by a means such as marketing, how can you ensure that person will return?

Ask yourself the following questions to see if you have the knowledge and behavior that encourages good word of mouth.

- Do you know how you can have an impact on your customers?
- Do you know how to measure weekly customer traffic, and whether or not the same customers return?
- Do you know your customers' expectations?
- Do you know when a customer is unhappy?

If you can guarantee you will impress your customers, and that they will recommend your business to their acquaintances, then we guarantee you will succeed. We can also guarantee that your ads will start working for you. However, remember that advertising does not do all the work for you; it only does the initial work. After that, your product or service must ensure your success.

Word of mouth is like a live, walking advertisement with emotions that connects with hundreds and thousands of people, who become a network of potential customers to whom information is sent personally.

Creating word-of-mouth advertising may not require you to significantly increase your investment in your business. Instead of spending all your money on newspaper ads, trade shows, events, radio stations, websites, and cable TV promotions, put your money directly into your business, so you can create in your specific market an experience that leads customers to speak well of your business.

**Personalized invitation**

Let's imagine two friends are in a shopping mall. As good friends, they know each other's tastes. One tells the other about a clothing store selling new pants that her friend would like; she describes the colors, patterns, and fabrics; the excellent customer service; the comfortable dressing rooms; the discount coupons. She is playing with her friend's emotions, and so her friend feels as if she must buy pants at that store.

If a potential customer asks somebody about a specific business because of a need to buy something, that we cannot call word-of-mouth advertising. Real word of mouth creates a personalized invitation only when a client feels excited and driven to tell someone else about your business.

You cannot control people outside your business. You can only control what happens within your business. Your main objective is to change your business so that it leaves such a deep and lasting impression on your customers, they must tell someone else.

And take care, because as potent and powerful as this tool is to create customer loyalty and attract a group of fans, it can also cause loss of customers and bad reputation.

## The franchise opportunity

There are various franchises in different types of markets, but the main value in franchises is in standardization and processes: how to open and close the store; how to decorate; how to display the merchandise; how employees should dress, behave and speak; how to cook; how to deliver a product; and how to measure service quality.

No matter what type of business you have, you can provide a customer with the same experience as a franchise, or close. You must give your customers a repeatable experience. They need to know what to expect from your business. They should have the same experience whenever they visit, and feel that you treat all customers equally.

Customer-focused service resides in the act of positioning your business to think about the customer as its principal objective. Design your processes, structures, products, and services with a customer focus. This seems logical to many, but we are sometimes amazed to observe during an evaluation how a company has designed its processes, products, and services in such a way as to make the customer suffer.

For example, a company sells a number of products for the home online. When a customer wishes to return a product, the steps or processes are designed so that:

- It will cost the customer more to ship the product than the product is worth.

- The product quality is bad, international shipping is paid by the customer, and the customer will only be refunded 40% of the original value.
- When a customer writes to the company, no answer is made until a week later, or perhaps ever.

This kind of business does not have customer-focused processes. Its processes are geared to sell once, with no thought towards encouraging a second sale.

Therefore, it is very important to review your business processes, perhaps with the help of a third party (to establish a customer membered focus group). Many business owners believe they are focused on meeting the needs of their customers, but this is just a delusion or a fantasy.

**First visualize the target, and then shoot**

If you open a business to satisfy your reasoning or your tastes, you are on your way to a battle that will be difficult, or that you may lose. But if you build your business based on a specific market, identifying what this market needs and what you can offer it, assessing whether the market has access to your business and the money to pay, then you are on the way to competition. If you can focus on the target market and also create a unique and incredible emotional experience, you are on the road to victory.

We will give you the following basic tips to achieve this:

- Keep your focus on the target.
- Observe the market reality with objectivity.
- Refine and update processes to match changes in the environment.
- Maintain a franchise philosophy in which the treatment of all customers is alike and repetitive.
- Be persistent and consistent in creating an environment where customers and employees are passionate about what they get and what they give.

In this way you will understand that having a global business vision allows you to see beyond a simple failure of marketing and advertising, and will open the door to sustained success without large investments of money, knowledge, and action.

**Strategies for turning your customers into partners**

**Target Market**

What is your target market? If you own a coffee shop, then would your target market be people who drink coffee?

When we talk about a target market, many people only think about the direct customer, which is fine. But we must widen our focus to a more comprehensive and global vision; that is, to see the environment that surrounds our goal. The idea is to *minimize effort and multiply resources*. When you learn to observe the infinite resources available in the environment and to connect them with the infinite possibilities that

the universe offers, you succeed in minimizing effort and creating a profound use of resources, resulting in a greater ability to penetrate the market.

We will explain this with the following example: in a store that sells video games, the target market is young people of perhaps eight to twenty years old, predominantly male, and advertising focuses exclusively on that group. But this advertising does not extend the scope of vision to what we call the second level.

This second level is to think about who else can buy the products, and what ways can be used to attract more groups of customers. In this case, the strategy will be to seek to attract the parents of these young men and seduce them with the idea that they too can play with their children; in the final analysis, it is really they who pay the money so the customer can buy the product.

The seller can also look for ways in which these potential customers are associated in order to capture groups. For example, it could be sports teams: a promotion of video games related to baseball, directed at students who play on baseball teams. It is this openness of ideas that will improve vision and market penetration. Once the seller has determined what this group (which in this case would be coaches and school teachers) is looking for, a campaign can be prepared and aimed at this sector or group which will generate more associations, and could be copied to use for another group of potential customers at the second level.

When we look at this example, we can determine several important features to keep in mind for the development of our target market, which can be expressed in **four steps**:

1. Identification of the principal market segment.

2. Identification of the second-level market segment.

3. Identification of possible ways of associating groups of potential customers.

4. Development of campaigns aimed at different levels and groups in a standard way that can be repeated, optimizing resources.

**STEP 1: Main Market (Business to consumer, or business to business)**

How can you do this? How can you put your business down on paper and generate a methodical plan that lets you view and open your vision of the target market at different levels?

We will define the target market towards which you want to focus your business. This market must have three key things: one is a need in the market that your product or service can satisfy; the second is easy access to your business; the third is an identification of the value of your service or product in exchange for the experience only you can provide. We will define your main target market:

**Geographic:**

Where is your business located? Do your customers have physical or virtual access to your business? What area of expansion do you want to penetrate?

_____

_____

**Demographic:**

Your customers' age, sex, race, ethnicity, marital status, family size, life cycle.

Their years in business, ownership, the decision-makers, their business cycle.

_____

_____

**Socioeconomic:**

Your customers' occupation, education, income.

Their goals in terms of sales, profits, marketing of their business.

_____

_____

**Psychographic:**

Your customers' lifestyle, personality, tastes.

Their corporate culture.  The values and mission of their business.

_____

_____

**Behavior:**

How do your customers act?  What do they respond to?  What are their likes and habits?  What do they do?

_____


_____


My customers buy:
- What?
- When?
- Where?
- How?
- Why?
- How much?
- How often?

The benefit from defining your target market is that you are able to see the trends, groups and types more clearly in order to determine the best way to serve and grow your business.  It is important to identify whether if your business is directly aimed at individuals or is focused on companies, because this determines how you should apply the tools we are presenting.

It is a question of all of the factors your customers take into consideration during the purchase process.

## STEP 2: Second-level market

To determine the second-level market, it is necessary to be clear about the principal market. You can use various existing techniques for the development of ideas, such as brainstorming calls, mind maps, etc. Any of these techniques will allow you to open the creative field in your mind that is often not used during the routine of everyday life. Remember that you are the person who knows your business best; only you have lived through all the critical and noncritical moments of your business; you have experienced the birth and growth of your business, as well as its stagnation. All these experiences are valuable, because that way you know which roads you have traveled that have failed, as well as those that have been successful.

On the other hand, it is important that this plan be developed as a team. If you have staff within your organization in various areas and there are people you know who are not involved in the business, but have the spark of creativity, you can form a multidisciplinary team to generate business ideas for the second-level market. It is always important to value differences, because often when we work as a team and a member thinks differently from the others, the normal human reaction is to immediately reject that person's input and not to provide the opportunity to express an idea that the "typical group" may not have seen. Valuing differences is a fundamental principle for teamwork and the generation of creative ideas for businesses.

Once you have generated the potential and the prospects for the second level, you can apply the questions from the previous step, with which you can determine the behavior of this new level of customers and thus move to the next step.

We will present a schematic table that allows you to describe the information for steps two and three in a structured form.

| Product / Service | Client (Level1, Level 2) | Group / Associations |
|---|---|---|
| Video games | Young 8-20 years old **(L1)** | |
| | Parents **(L2)** | Group of parents |
| | Coaches **(L2)** | Baseball Teams |

**STEP 3: Access to groups and associations**

In the same way we used brainstorming tools to determine second-level customers, we can apply them in identifying groups or associations that will allow us to optimize effort. Think for a moment about how your current advertising medium works on one person and how much it is costing you to use this medium, in money as well as in time and effort. The idea is to optimize resources, to try to make your advertising reach masses and groups, and often this route will be more economical than the traditional way.

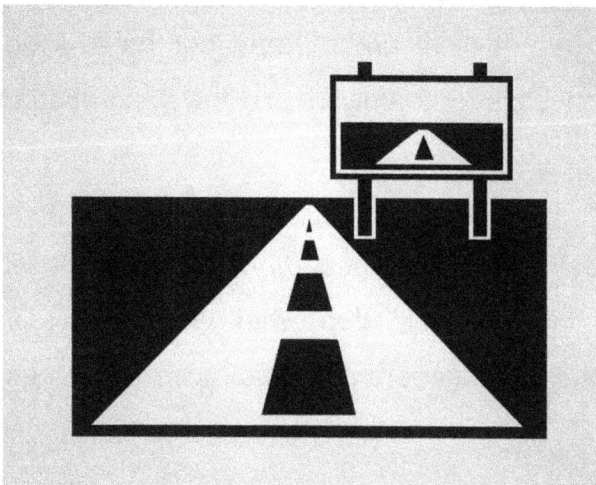

When you analyze what your customers do, what their habits are, how they feel before and after using your product or service, their expectations, then you should understand, you should feel that you are in their shoes; and once you feel this deeply, you can make the connection regarding how to relate to groups or associations.

There is a mental process that we must understand as business owners. It may sound strange at first, but later you will understand it. You feel that your business simply offers a good product or service that is within reach of your customer. That sounds good, it could cover any business and keep it in business; but if I say now that you should **see your customer as a potential business partner**, you could say at first that it is not possible, because your customer is not in business to sell goods or services of any kind. But this is the key to your business; when you see your client as a partner, then you can visualize the way to make alliances with groups or associations.

The following example illustrates how a change in viewing the client makes a business grow and attract great opportunities using minimal resources:

Carlos has a gym in a residential area north of the city. He decided to change his marketing strategy to attract more customers. He began to see his customers as partners, offering them a membership card that gives them discounts on their monthly fees if they bring new customers to the business. Additionally, he offered membership packages to corporate groups in which executives and employees get certain benefits if they enter into the association or group. He also generated lines of business directed at the elderly, retirees, and groups of therapists. In this way he created and duplicated an advertising campaign without having to spend a large amount of money for it, and he multiplied his business exponentially.

As you can see, the main point is to determine:
- The product package/service you want to promote.
- Who the groups or associations are.
- The method or way to reach these groups.

With these three clear elements, you can supplement the above table and thus have the information better structured in order to move to the last step, which is the development of the campaign.

You can then use the following table to develop your business.

## STEP 4: Develop campaigns

To develop a campaign, you need the above information, in addition to a focus on a standard approach. In other words, as you develop the first advertising campaign focused on the first package of products/services for a given association, think about what might work for the second and third levels of your list in a way that simplifies your efforts and saves resources.

It is also important to consider communication methods and social media, for through these you can reach large numbers of people and groups, and in many cases they are free or inexpensive.

Another important element is to value the people, organizations and groups to which you are affiliated or that you must join. Participating in chambers of commerce and in industry, and attending events and training, allows you to meet people; and these connections also function as a means of marketing your business, as in the familiar expression "hit the street." It is important to use both electronic media and human contact.

A campaign can have different structures and designs. The way to prepare an advertising campaign is well-documented in books and on the Internet, but the interesting thing is to connect all the information in the tables above and put it into practice. Remember that an idea without action is nothing.

You can schedule your campaigns in periods, and in this way you will have a controlled program that you can keep track of over time, as you should be measuring the results the campaign produces as you proceed, taking measurements on the path and making adjustments. Remember that you will not create a infallible program; this program can be changed and can be adjusted as it is implemented, and this way you will not have the sensation of waiting until the end to see the results.

To make the road shorter, you already have an analysis of your product and of the path where you can direct it; now you will develop how you will do it, and put action and passion into the implementation (see campaign form on next page).

| CAMPAIGN NAME | | | FREQUENCY | |
|---|---|---|---|---|
| DESCRIPTION | | | | |
| INNOVATION | | | | |
| GROUP / ASSOCIATIONS | | CONNECTION | | |
| BENEFICS | CLIENT | | ORGANIZATION | |
| | | | | |
| | | | | |
| | | | | |
| RESOURCE | | | | |

| PROGRAM | | | | |
|---|---|---|---|---|
| ACTIVITIES | RESOURCE | COSTS | START DATE | END DATE |
| | | | | |
| | | | | |
| | | | | |
| | | | | |
| | | | | |
| | | | | |
| | | | | |

CHAPTER 9 (Day 55)

## Prepare Your Independent Sellers

When an organization starts to develop in the area of sales, there is usually a lack of knowledge about and resources for hiring permanent employees. At this point, the business owners are afraid they might lose their financial investment, during a process that can take months or years with no reward at the end for the money and time invested.

In this situation, you cannot dismiss the idea of establishing a strategy of hiring independent retailers, in that the investment of money is minimal and the risks are distributed between both parties, the seller and the organization.

The goal to be achieved in this chapter is to provide tools to the business owner or the head of marketing and sales in order to establish a plan and put it into practice, to hire independent vendors with the necessary controls that enable them to make a win-win alliance for both parties.

This not only involves establishing a plan but also implementing the rules of the game, since in commercial agreements it is very important to be clear about what procedures, rules, and guidelines are to be followed, and what the parties' conditions are.

The importance of this extends from the moment you determine the services or products that require marketing, the pricing, the commissions, up until the close of the sales process.

## DESCRIPTION OF THE PROCESS

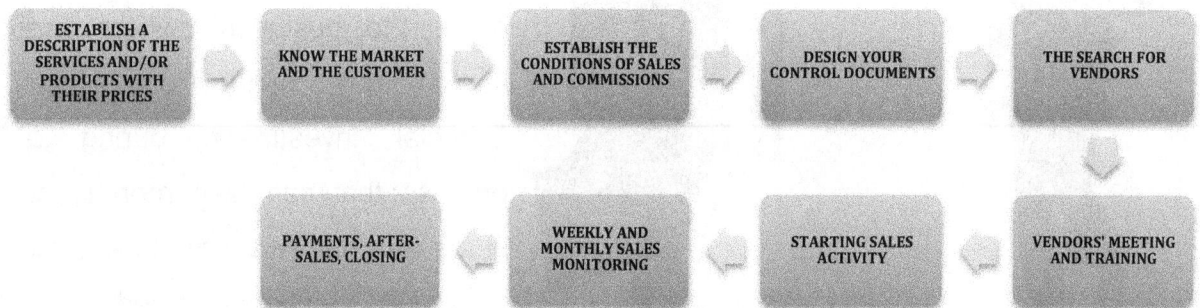

| ESTABLISH A DESCRIPTION OF THE SERVICES AND/OR PRODUCTS WITH THEIR PRICES | KNOW THE MARKET AND THE CUSTOMER | ESTABLISH THE CONDITIONS OF SALES AND COMMISSIONS | DESIGN YOUR CONTROL DOCUMENTS | THE SEARCH FOR VENDORS |
|---|---|---|---|---|
| PAYMENTS, AFTER-SALES, CLOSING | WEEKLY AND MONTHLY SALES MONITORING | STARTING SALES ACTIVITY | VENDORS' MEETING AND TRAINING | |

## ESTABLISH A DESCRIPTION OF THE SERVICES AND/OR PRODUCTS WITH THEIR PRICES

A clear and specific description of the products and services is essential to initiate this process, as it provides the necessary routes for both the seller and the organization to have the tools for establishing a positive strategic market plan.

Many organizations establish these sales activities intuitively or by custom and experience, without having a specific and clear method for implementing a good sales and marketing campaign.

Sometimes this is where sales energy dissipates and productivity is lost, because the market gets worn out, and it seems you invest time and money in marketing and sales with a minimal return on investment.

The need to clearly describe your product and service is not simply so that your potential client hears and understands it. This description allows you as a connoisseur of your business to open ideas in the place your product and service is directed towards.

We will explain with the following example: suppose I sell tropical fruit, and my business simply looks for fruit from suppliers and sells it to small shops. When I focus on believing that I am just a distributor of fruit, I do not see the range of options the business can offer. However, in describing my activities as guided by this method, I will see a wide range of opportunities I may not have previously observed. For example:

- I look for the best suppliers with good-quality, low-priced fruit.
- I establish the best ways to have an easy and practical route, saving time and money in distribution.
- I select, classify and maintain customers who pay on time and I have good relationships with them.
- I control my resources, such as my vehicle, personnel, and legal aspects, to achieve an excellent service and product.

Note that the activities carried out are clearly described in four sentences, and not with a simple phrase such as: "I am a seller of tropical fruit."

What do these four sentences allow us to do? With them we can develop and open a panorama of endless opportunities, and we will explain how:

SENTENCE 1:  *"I look for the best suppliers with good-quality, low-priced fruit."*

*1.  Where are my suppliers located?  Is it easy to get there?  Are they all in one place?  Should I move somewhere else?*

*2.  Do I really evaluate the quality of the fruit?  When I receive damaged fruit, does the supplier replace it?  Is the price of the fruit fair, compared to its value? Relative to the market, is the price competitive?*

*3.  Do I know my competition's prices?  Do I know the prices of other fruit suppliers, and where I can find new suppliers?*

With the first description, you can generate a series of questions and answers that opens the door to seeing another picture of your products or services.

This technique allows you to better describe the activities you do and in turn leads to analyzing how, what, where, when, and why.  This information will open doors in your mind that will help you in the next two steps, which are:  knowing the market and setting the terms of sale.

In the same way you applied this technique to the first sentence of the description, you should apply it to the following ones, and you will have excellent material.

**SET PRICES**

On the subject of pricing, it is important to know a simple formula that can be applied when you know the fixed and variable costs of the business.

**Price = Fixed Costs + Variable Costs + Profit**

To determine the costs and their types, you must be very well organized in terms of how costs are being dealt with in the organization.

Below is a simple list.

**a) Fixed Costs**

These costs remain constant regardless of the level of activity of the organization. For example:

1. Rentals.
2. Utilities (power, internet, telephone, gas, etc.).
3. Depreciation of equipment.
4. Insurance.
5. Fixed taxes.
6. Salary and wages.

## b) Variable Costs

These costs vary according to the level of production or activity of the organization. For example:

- Direct manpower hired specifically for production.
- Direct raw materials.
- Direct materials and supplies.
- Specific taxes.
- Containers, packaging, shipping and labels.
- Sales commissions.

## c) Profit

To determine profit, you must take into account the **unit cost** of your product or service, which is the sum of fixed and variable costs divided by production. In some cases, if we provide diverse services it is very difficult to establish this parameter, but we can manage the value in man-hours invested to accomplish production.

You should check the prices of the competition and similar products or services and use them as a reference standard.

You must know what additional value your product or service has with respect to the competition, and what the market requires. This additional value lets you establish a higher or lower worth that ensures the market will purchase your product or service.

Once you know your fixed and variable costs, and determine what the market is like, you can establish a percentage or a whole number of profit that fits the business and which you can later use to maintain and grow your business.

## KNOW THE MARKET AND THE CUSTOMER

In this step, it is important to know specifically the benefits, strengths, and weaknesses of your service and/or product, because these form part of the foundation for the customer to whom you want to sell and the type of market in which you are focused.

Knowing the target customer is not easy, as many people find after investing a lot of time and money. But having a basic description of what the customer does, the service provided, the product that is generated, saves you from investing some time and money.

To describe the target customer to whom you want to sell, you need to document and find techniques that will allow you access to key business points. Here are a few simple questions to help you specify:

- What are the habits of the customer who may need your product?
- According to your price, what economic sector are you aiming at?
- According to style, at what personal, professional, industrial, commercial profile?
- At what gender, age, culture?
- According to your scope, at what geographic area?

With these questions, and the exercise you completed in the previous chapter, you can better visualize your customer and the market where you want to take your service or product.

It is also advisable to revisit your competition, as you will notice if you are a pioneer with your proposal or are in a market where the same product/service abounds. You should also know how to compete in that market either by changes to your product/service or price level, or by offering some "added value" that differentiates you from the competition.

Another element to analyze is substitute or complementary products/services that may not be direct competition, but are taking part of your market.

## ESTABLISH THE CONDITIONS OF SALES AND COMMISSIONS

Before going out to look for sellers, it is necessary to know the conditions and commissions, as this shows you what type and level of people you need to put into action in your business.

Setting the ground rules is a fundamental task in this area, especially with the bad habit that many people have of making solely verbal economic agreements, which can eventually cause personal, labor, financial, legal, and even health problems.

To make this step easy and simple, the first thing to do is set the amount or percentage of commission you are willing to pay vendors. Generally these percentages range between 1% and 20%; but this value depends on the type of business and will usually be an initial number that can vary as the seller progresses, in order to provide goals to be achieved.

These percentages or fixed amounts can also vary depending on the type of product/service you want to market, since in many cases if you have a product/service that is easy to sell in large quantities, you may establish a low percentage. For a difficult or exclusive one, you could establish a high percentage that is balanced with the seller's efforts.

Designing clear, simple, and precise conditions permits a comfortable environment for both the seller and the manager or leader of the organization conducting the activity.

One of the best ways to control this activity is to make a list of the points described below, that you can use to prepare this instrument of agreement.

Example:

**AGREEMENT FOR SELLERS**

1. Prepare documentation with the following information:
   - Announcements, data sheets, advertising describing the service or product.
   - Monthly calendar showing promotional activities, meetings, offers, events, etc.
   - Special promotional packages, samples of products or services, testimonials, recommendations from other customers, etc.
   - Business cards.
   - Descriptive inventory of all products or services as an easily accessible summary list.
   - A written agreement between the parties.
2. Terms of agreement:

- Scope of the market, or area that will be subject to marketing and sales.
- Clear percentages for products or services.
- Conditions for cancellation of the commission, time, where, when, elements not covered by the commission.
- Benefits of being a seller, such as enjoying special discounts according to set time or goals.
- Table showing sales goals over time, both in money and in quantities, that allows challenges between vendors.
- Special bonuses.
- Values and ethics managed by the business to preserve its image.

Once you have this information documented and physically prepared in an orderly and attractive way, you can go on to the next activity, confident of minimizing disagreements and issues that can bring future problems.

This documentation must be reviewed every month, as it is normal for there to be changes as it is being used, and in this way you are guaranteed to be covered against possible eventualities.

Create the habit of having weekly and monthly control meetings in order to have a system of continuous improvement.

## DESIGN YOUR CONTROL DOCUMENTS

Every process within an organization requires controls to ensure its operation. The control element should be simple, appropriate, and easy to implement so that it does not obstruct the proper functioning of the process.

As experts in process control design, we can tell you that one of the key features is that it is easy to implement and attractive to the user. When a control is not appealing to the user, it starts to be evaded and infringed upon, and becomes more of a problem than a help.

For the control of independent vendors, we have established the following points:

- Sellers' agreement.
- Registration table for prospects and customers.
- Schedule, visit control, communication, campaigns.
- Control of sales and commissions.

The important thing is how to adjust and implement these controls, because step-by-step we are providing tools for establishing a successful strategy that will allow you to assess and control your management.

## RECOMMENDATIONS FOR EACH DOCUMENT

Sellers' agreement

You can find many examples on the Internet. What is necessary is that this document should be designed and revised to remove or add terms and conditions depending on your business, and the agreements you wish to establish. Once you have the agreement ready and have the data filled in for each vendor, it must be submitted for review and discussion by the parties. Once both parties agree and make the necessary changes to the document, it should be printed and signed in two originals, one for the seller and one for the company.

## Registration table for prospects and customers

This is a document that can be completed digitally or on paper. The idea of this document is to record potential prospects you are going to visit and have visited. This document should be used both to prepare a preliminary list of potential customers you want to visit, as well as after the visit to record the information gathered and any requirements that the prospect has.

The importance of this paper is that it has several final aims: it allows you to generate a database of prospects, to monitor vendor activities, and to take maximum advantage of an instrument of control for following up on the agreements between the prospect and the seller in terms of presenting offers.

## Schedule, visit control

The schedule is variable; the seller can use any scheduling tool, whether a phone, electronic agenda, diary, paper sheets, etc. The purpose is not only to control the plan of visits the vendor should make, but also to measure the effectiveness of the plan compared to reality.

Control visits may be integrated into the schedule or may be a separate document, but to generate more trust they should be signed by the prospect or potential client in order to provide evidence of the work done by the seller.

## Communication, campaigns

You need to deliver, and to place in your document portfolio, copies of any internal organizational communications related to conditions of the product/service that may affect the seller's work in the field. It is also important to give the seller details of the scope of any campaigns and promotions that the organization may be establishing.

Control of sales and commissions

This document can be completed electronically or on paper. It records sales made daily, or as often as you wish them to be recorded. This document counts the sales for each vendor and the established commission conditions in order to fulfill them to vendors.

This control commission has two forms: the **Sales Control Form** that will be for the use of the seller and the company, where the seller records sales and the company certifies them; and the **Commission Control Form**, where the company collects data about all vendors and all sales, and so can analyze in depth how the products/services and the sellers themselves are doing. It also lets you know the amount of money to be managed in terms of fees payable, bonuses, and other agreements.

**THE SEARCH FOR VENDORS**

The task of searching for vendors can be as easy or difficult as you can imagine. If you do not have the previous points established, you will not be able to know the features and qualities of the seller's profile, and much less will you be able to show the seller your market potential.

It is not attractive for most independent sellers to start working in an organization where there is no salary or regular payment. Additionally, having "independence"

148

makes the organization feel they have no control. All these elements play an important role in the understanding of both parties to the contract, since the contractor must be able to explain the wonderful opportunities that the independent seller has and not focus exclusively on a wage or salary.

Successful salespeople know that commissions are the interesting part of the world of sales, even though there are basic promotional costs. These promotional expenses should be well analyzed by the company, because whether or not you will need to set amounts for transportation, telephone, or any other basic, necessary related costs depends on what you want to establish and the areas to be covered.

At this point, we can play with many aspects, and it all depends on:
- The type of business.
- The resources available for sellers.
- An attractive commission package.
- Commitment and good business presentation to vendors.
- A clearly designed profile of the market and the vendor.

With all these points developed, you can design a good vendor search plan, following these steps:

a) Design of the vendor profile

For the design of the profile, you should make a list of essential features that you think the seller should have, in personal, professional, and experiential areas. You can rely on the Position Description that you created earlier, and focus it on your product/service. This way you can be more specific, but not limited in the vendor search.

90 Day Challenge

b) Design of the vendor search ad

From the profile information, you can take some phrases and keywords that should be placed in the ad. It is important that the ad has the logo and name of your organization; this will give it an aspect that will interest the vendors. Even if your company is very small, placing the name of the organization in the ad will make the candidate feel interested in participating in recruitment. Establish specific e-mail and mailing addresses where people can physically and electronically send résumés.

c) List of methods of publication

Depending on the area, location, and profile of the seller, the places where the search is publicized should be varied. You can use digital social media and public places such as libraries, clubs, sports centers, shopping centers, and meeting centers. Use whatever is permitted by each method that gives you access to the public at the level or in the area where you are looking. You can also use the regular ways such as press, radio, magazines, headhunters' websites, etc.

d) Receipt and classification of résumés

Once you have the résumés, you must set a filter to sort them from highest to lowest preference, in order to begin the interviews. Depending on the number of vendors you want and how many résumés you receive, you should sort so that you have a minimum of three people for each position. If you have time, try to interview up to five in order to have more room for decision-making.

e) Interview process

For the interview process to be productive, it is recommended that more than one person in the organization assist in the selection. In this way, in one day, two or more people in the company will be dedicated to summoning the candidates at different times, and will have to spend a maximum of one hour on each candidate. In other words, depending on the candidates, interviews will be finished in three to five hours.

f) Selection and recruitment process

Once you finish the interviews, it is important to discuss the results and determine the best candidate for the job. Remember that the selection process is a major cause of high staff turnover in an organization. The consequences of a poor choice are the loss of money, time, and resources that could have been saved if a good selection process had been established. Remember, a person's attitude can outweigh any experience, profession, or technical knowledge. It is important to know well who you want to represent your business in the street; to know who will create the image your customers have of your organization.

As for recruitment, you must present every detail established in the "Vendor Agreement" to the seller. Both parties must agree to that document, and it must be signed and distributed between the parties.

# VENDORS' MEETING AND TRAINING

Once the vendors are hired, it is necessary to perform training and induction so they will clearly know both the organization and the services and products it provides. This type of training can vary depending on the complexity of your marketing plan. But the more effective and shorter this process, the sooner you can have people ready to take the field of battle.

The organization's key people need to be present at the meeting, along with operational staff who have contact with sellers.

Topics to be addressed at the meeting are:
- Presentation of company personnel.
- Mission, vision, and goals of the company.
- Establishment of sales goals, areas, products/services.
- Terms and general rules of the organization.
- Schedules, uniforms, image, logos, documents, work material.
- Delivery of material for sale.
- Motivational speech.
- Presentation of the control documents.
- Vendors' convention.
- Registration table for prospects and customers.
- Schedule, visit control, communication, campaigns.
- Control of sales and commissions.
- Question and answer session.

After holding the initial meeting, one week of training and induction can be set, so that vendors will have time to adapt to the organization and learn more about the company.

The induction process should include:

## 1. The company

    1.1  Presentation of sales material (a folder describing products, services, and promotions).

    1.2  Management of the company's values, mission, and vision.

    1.3  Establishment of objectives and goals, and monitoring practice.

    1.4  Establishment of routes, plans, schedule.

    1.5  Communication policies: e-mail, phone, meetings.

## 2. Services and products

    2.1  Knowledge of product lines.

    2.2  Release technique (how service delivery is coordinated).

    2.3  Administrative and operational aspects of service delivery.

## 3. Internal procedures (practice)

    3.1  Payment of per diem and expenses.  Payment form.

    3.2  Control of commission payments.  Forms.

    3.3  Control and management of customer contracts.  Forms.

    3.4  Control and reduction of bonuses. Practice.

    3.5  Management and correct use of price list.

    3.6  Management of information sheets for customer complaints.

    3.7  Management of supervisors' reports.

## 4. External procedures

4.1 External procedures. Practice with supervisor.

4.2 Client contact and the selling process.

4.3 Basic steps of the sale. Practice with supervisor.

4.4 Proof that the seller has contacted a customer.

## STARTING SALES ACTIVITY

Once the seller has gone through induction, after one or two weeks, start the sales process, in which the vendor must go out alone in search of customers, keeping in mind the targets set in the previous step.

It is essential to set goals for the sales process, because simply going out to sell without having a final goal in mind can be a waste of time and resources. In sales activity, monitoring and control is needed that allows the organization to monitor the activity and the vendor, and that will be an instrument of measurement to show the seller's work.

In any business, the first months of sales are not that successful, since it is necessary to know the market, customer behavior, and ways to make contacts. A great range of opportunities can be opened, and much depends on the skills and creativity of the seller. This guide helps greatly to establish order in terms of sales administration, but the way vendors seek diverse alternatives to become more successful will largely depend on them. You can find information in our business kits such as: "Design your Business Marketing", "Strategies for Turning your Customers into Partners", and "Partnerships with the Competition". In these kits, you can find better ways for dealing with any type of market with new tools, innovative strategies, and tactics that are easy and inexpensive to apply to your business.

You can also search our website, http://90daysolutions.com/, where there is always updated information and you can ask any questions that you have.

The start of sales activity should incorporate several principles, such as:

- Regularity of the weekly meetings in terms of day and time. Make this a routine practice within the organization.
- Constant contact by phone, e-mail, etc. between the vendor and the supervisor or person representing the company.
- The sales offers submitted by the vendor to the company should be carried out as soon as possible and delivered to the customer on the agreed date.
- The vendor should feel constantly supported by the organization.
- The vendor's image should be protected, because it is part of the company even though the seller is considered independent.
- Control and monitoring should be handled with care, and should be both subtle and constant.

## WEEKLY AND MONTHLY SALES MONITORING

With the implementation of the control documents we have provided, you can keep track of sales. In turn, these controls may provide valuable information both for managing the seller and for awareness of market performance, keeping a database of prospects and customers. Controlled and continuous monitoring is the best way to determine whether something is working or not.

In the world of sales and with the diversity of sellers' attitudes, they may present different types of characters that can create a smoke screen between reality and fantasy. Many sellers know the art of enthralling people, and they can often do this with the company they work for. For this reason, it is important to establish clear rules from the beginning, as the issue of control and monitoring is not an attractive element to them, since they consider sales to be an art that can lose inspiration when controls are placed on it.

In these cases, if the company puts the rules of the game on the table from the very beginning, creates an accord and signs the agreement, this will present control as part of the wonderful art of selling via monitoring and control techniques, without losing the magic that the vendors speak of.

The control of weekly visits, the number of offers made, and closing sales are numbers that must be managed and monitored weekly.

For example, if you establish the goal that the seller must visit at least eight potential customers a week, these eight possible customers may require four or five business offers or bids, which may represent one or two sales per week. With this method, the seller will be able to experiment with sales techniques that allow him or her to establish an offer, and the way to present it so that it can become a sale.

When using the "Control of weekly visits," and the "Registration table for prospects and customers", these two documents should be updated daily and presented at the weekly meeting for review and discussion among the vendors and the organization.

At the end of the month it is important to have the total numbers for the entire management:

- Number of visits.
- Number of offers submitted.
- Number of sales.
- Total services/products sold.
- Total amount sold per month.
- Total commissions payable.
- Bonuses and other benefits.

At weekly meetings, it is important to keep these figures in mind, and how near or far you are from reaching the goal. This may change over time depending on the behavior of the numbers and the market. It is also important to check the strategies used and to discuss them within the group of vendors so you can have information feedback among each vendor, the organization, and the market.

**PAYMENTS, AFTER-SALES, CLOSING**

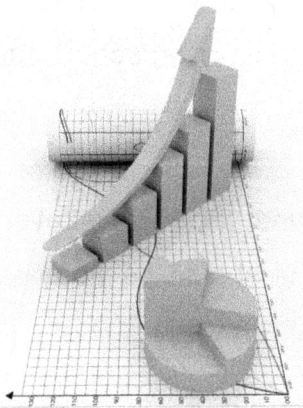

Payments to vendors should be made on the date agreed to in the contract. It is vital that the organization behave responsibly in terms of this settlement, because an unmotivated seller who feels cheated by an agreement can be very dangerous for the organization.

It is necessary to foresee cases where the organization has not yet collected some sales invoices, so that this does not affect the agreement with the seller. With good financial management and control of payments, it will be possible to have a good working environment that ensures harmony in this system of independent sellers.

The after-sales process includes activities where the seller depends on the client to confirm satisfaction with the product/service purchased. Remember that a satisfied customer can grow your business exponentially, and that most sales are made based on recommendations from satisfied customers. But a dissatisfied customer is just as powerful, and may destroy much of your business if you do not take a complaint into consideration.

The organization must have methods of controlling the complaints and claims of customers. In this case, sellers are once again a means of communication between the customer and the organization.

When closing sales are achieved and the corresponding payments are made, it is important to have an added bonus system that can be managed with figures such as top salesman of the month, the one who brought in the most offers, the one who rescued a market, the one who sold the most of a particular type of product, etc. This kind of recognition creates a healthy environment of competition and challenges within the organization that converts the business into a passionate place for sellers.

## PROSPECTS AND CUSTOMERS RECORDS

| VISIT DATE | CLIENT NAME | CONTACT | ADDRESS, PHONE | E-MAIL | REQUIREMENT | DELIVERY OFFER DATE | SIGN |
|---|---|---|---|---|---|---|---|
|  |  |  |  |  |  |  |  |
|  |  |  |  |  |  |  |  |
|  |  |  |  |  |  |  |  |
|  |  |  |  |  |  |  |  |
|  |  |  |  |  |  |  |  |
|  |  |  |  |  |  |  |  |
|  |  |  |  |  |  |  |  |
|  |  |  |  |  |  |  |  |

## VISIT CONTROL

| CLIENT NAME | PLAN VISIT DATE | REAL VISIT DATE | ADDRESS, PHONE | AGREEMENTS | WHY NOT VISIT | NEXT VISIT DATE | SIGN |
|---|---|---|---|---|---|---|---|
| | | | | | | | |
| | | | | | | | |
| | | | | | | | |
| | | | | | | | |
| | | | | | | | |
| | | | | | | | |
| | | | | | | | |

90 Day Challenge

## CHAPTER 10 (DAY 75)

## Plan, Control, and Monitor

When it comes to planning and control, we can present an entire treatise with information on how to do it, but the most important point here is how you conceive the concept of planning, controlling, and monitoring (PCM). These are the factors that can enable you to complete your vision, mission and objectives. There is no value to all the elements we have described and worked on in the previous days, if there is no planning, control, and monitoring of each activity over time.

This must become for you not only a concept for managing activities; it should be part of your life, your beliefs, and your attitude. With years of experience we have developed projects, both on paper and in physical implementation, in which we were able to direct the planning and execution of large-scale projects such as the installation of a gas processing plant in just eight months, from the breaking of the ground to the point where all the facilities were functioning as offices, including recreation areas. Because we have this experience, we understand how a good plan, coupled with well-defined control and daily monitoring of each of the activities that took place, were the secret to achieving great things in a short time and with costs well-structured so that each activity was productive and efficient.

This type of example could make you think, "*yes, but they had all the resources at hand, which is why they succeeded.*" We can say that we have been involved in other projects where all resources were at hand and completion was not achieved in time, and there was even a waste of money and resources. The point here is the ability to see each element, be it resources, knowledge, order, plan, discipline, or method. Another important point is that the leader of the group understands that he or she must comply with the plan, of course, if the plan is well-designed.

In this chapter we want to awaken you to the value and attitude of managing and controlling a plan. We know that not everything in life can be planned, but it is important to know what things you must plan for, and to do it.

Let's not leave decisions that are our responsibility in the hands of fate, or blame the environment for what has happened to us in our organization and much less in our lives. What we need you to understand is how to take these elements as an instrument or vital tool for your business.

One of the principal characteristics of planning, control, and monitoring (PCM) is the links between each element that make them work in a productive way. We want to take this information into the cells of your mind so that you act with the greatest possible consciousness. Let us compare this concept of PCM with the behavior of DNA, where each DNA compound consists of many simple units connected to each other, like a train made up of many cars, and the information traveling on that train is the genetic coding. This genetic information affects your entire body, both physically and mentally. In the same way, when PCM is malfunctioning, problems are triggered that will affect your entire organization.

Describing the concept of DNA gives us a basis for the concept of PCM as a systematic process with interrelated elements that can be used to achieve a specific goal or objective. Each of these elements contains information that can be copied, reproduced, and implemented for self-improvement and transformation.

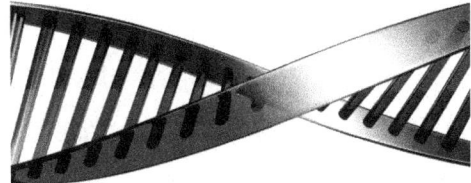

To expand this concept, imagine routine planning in which each resource involved (time, materials, equipment, people) is linked to an activity that can be put into practice and evaluated constantly, and in which each resource has information recorded from the vision and objective to be achieved to ensure effective use and optimization. This process may also have the capacity to self-generate information, to the extent that activities are being managed and put into practice, thus achieving transformation and redefinition.

When we talk about transformation and redefinition of an element, this can apply to an organization, a home, a society. It is the process from which there is no return, where the change is so profound and comprehensive that each element involved is affected and the change warrants a new definition: "redefinition".

Once you understand this concept and you introduce it into the DNA of your mind and cells, we can give you practical tools for use and action.

**PLANNING PRINCIPLES**

In the first chapter, we have provided techniques for managing the 90-day plan, and a weekly plan that allows you to monitor the behavior of what has been achieved or not, and to analyze the causes. That first exercise and your compliance will create the habit of control and monitoring. Now let's reinforce how to use the same method on the operational side of the organization, the projects, and any new challenge undertaken such as advertising campaigns, internal campaigns for improvement, etc. This tool can be used in different areas.

Here is a list of principles to follow:
- Clearly define the needs involved in the plan to be undertaken.
- Identify the activities involved in reaching the goal you desire.
- Sort the activities by type, performance levels, chronologically, however you think it best to tackle them.
- Set the duration of the activities.
- Establish the priorities of the activities in time.
- Establish the responsible persons involved in the activities.
- Determine the resources associated with the activities, whether material, labor, equipment, money, etc.
- Determine precedence links between one activity and another. This refers to activities that can be performed concurrently or that depend on other activities; that is to say, after one is finished, another begins.
- Check whether the activities are well-detailed or warrant creating task forces to do this so that the activity is achieved.
- Take into account the possible interruptions, delays, and inconveniences.
- When an activity is very complex, divide it into several simple tasks.
- Determine when follow-ups will be performed and how they will be done.

- Check that everyone understands the scope of the responsibilities outlined in the plan.
- Establish criteria and rules for re-planning, date changes, changes of responsibility, changes of priorities, etc.
- Rely on technology adapted for use in planning and monitoring.

## PRINCIPLES FOR CONTROL AND MONITORING

The establishment of control and monitoring for your plan should become a habit, with which every day or even several times a day you can measure the progress or otherwise of the planned activities. This is not to say that you will live with a checklist in your hand, following up all day; but to create this habit, you must use various techniques that will become customary in your mind when you understand how things are going in your organization.

If you are one of those people who often forgets pending items, then schedule management and a checklist will be of great help. You can keep it handy with the use of technology, whether by using your phone, your computer, or any other device. If you are not very fond of technology, use paper, which will similarly help you with tracking control.

Control can be a tedious task, but see it as a measuring instrument, as if it were a physical device like a thermometer that you place in different areas to check the temperature and see if all goes well or if you should start opening windows, close them, or lower the temperature of the air conditioning or heating. Your mind must understand that it is a mechanism for measuring the organization's performance without imposing emotional burdens that cause problems in the organization, whether with partners or employees.

Among some principles to follow are:

- Establishment of control criteria. Here you should clarify the frequency, and type of data to be controlled while following the plan. A criterion can range from the design of a data collection form completed daily, weekly, or on a schedule that you set, to the comparison of the plan to what was achieved.

- Establish the frequency and scope of control, including where and when it occurs.

- The independence of control: that there is no conflict of interest involving the person gathering the information or the person who analyzes it, because lack of objectivity with the data is not helpful to the organization.

- Hold meetings, interviews, tours, because these are also monitoring and control techniques.

- Control the variables related to planning, such as costs, time, and resources, in an independent way so that you get a better analysis of the parts.

- Determine which tasks are critical for the implementation of activities and fulfillment of the plan, and which are not.

- Give greater importance to, and take greater control of, critical tasks in order to optimize resources.

- Take corrective actions immediately in order to avoid delays in the completion of tasks.

- Make general revisions to the original plan, and adjust it if necessary to optimize it.

- Involve other people who can have an auditor's vision towards monitoring and control.

- Make changes to resources, whether by adding or removing labor, materials, equipment, time, or money.

- Analyze deviations from the plan and turn them into learning.

- Make decisions based on the data and not on emotion.

- Be careful not to accelerate or slow down any activity on a whim.

- When you need to change priorities, ask yourself if that activity affects other people, and make the best decision.

- Make projections of situations to identify the possible risks and to consider alternative plans or contingency plans.

- Always have a contingency plan at hand for critical activities, and know when to use it.

- Maintain open communication among members of the plan, so that everyone knows how activities are going and has the monitoring and control data.

- Hold regular meetings to discuss progress.

- When the plan is delayed, you must recognize it; failure to do so will not help. Recognize it and take action.

- Use negotiation techniques in those cases where delays are due to the human factor, and seek to unite rather than divide.

- Postponing decision-making will not help the progress of the plan.

- Take care to ensure good communication (Chapter 4).

- Take care of interpersonal relationships.

## Time Management

Time is interpreted differently by everyone. The perception of time for each person is a mystery that is reflected in the results of their lives. When we make comments indicating that one person has more time than another, it seems we believe one person has some twenty or thirty hours per day and another has

only twenty-four. We all have the same amount of time; the point is how you use the twenty-four hours that you have each day.

There are others who use the typical phrase: *"Yes, I'll do it later."* When is later? The fact of indicating an infinite space for your goal makes it unattainable, or simply makes you work faster as *later* turns into *hurry, there is no more time.* With simple examples, we can recreate this ghost that exists in your mind with regard to the time.

Later can be thirty minutes afterwards, an hour, a day; how much later? If, on the contrary, you answer: *"I will do it before 4 pm"*, or *"I will do it in an hour"*, your mind activates itself to finish what you are doing right now, and is ready to finish the agreement as established. There are other phrases like: *one day*, *perhaps, I might do it*; in short, all these sentences do not allow us to be as productive as we need to be.

Then you can think about what you are doing that causes delay in your activities: What is not working well? Is it that the method I'm using does not work? Is it because I have too many distractions, or because I'm trying to do more than I'm able to?

There are three terms in the management of productive work that should be mentioned. They are:

1. Core content.
2. Supplemental content.
3. Downtime.

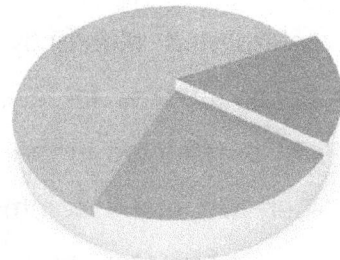

1. **Core content:**  The minimum time needed to perform the work under required conditions; in other words, the work needed to run the business without interruption.

2. **Supplemental content:**  The time needed to prepare all the materials, equipment, documents, whatever resource you need to do the work or core content.  This includes searching for information, adjusting equipment, tools that are not available.  It is all the time that is not productive but is necessary to prepare for production.

3. **Downtime:**  The time in which people, equipment, or machinery are inactive due to deficiencies of any kind, whether lack of planning, changes in plans, damaged equipment, accidents, absences, delays, distractions, etc.

The point here is to try to reduce as much as possible the time invested in supplemental content and downtime.  In this way, you will invest the most time into core content, allowing you to be more productive and efficient.

Below, you will perform an exercise that will allow you to better assess your time management and thus achieve the efficiency you need.

**Exercise:**

Make a list of the activities you performed yesterday or on a busy day that you feel are important to analyze.  Develop a chronological list specifying the tasks or activities done every thirty minutes or every hour.

Then identify which activities are core content, which are supplemental content, and which are downtime.

Once you determine the time spent doing each of these three groups of activities, indicate the total time per day and the percentage that corresponds to each group.

In this way you can determine whether your work day was really productive or not.

**Result:** Core content should occupy more than 60% of the time in a day, supplemental content should be approximately 25%, and downtime less than 15%.

## REMOVING THE CAUSES

To get rid of a problem, you should examine its root cause. With the exercise above, you were able to see where you are investing your time and whether that way of investing it is giving you the results you are experiencing in your business and in your personal life, family life, and even your health.

First you must understand that **time is limited** and not infinite, that the activities **are priorities**, and that everything depends on how you **plan your time**.

**Setting priorities:** Unfortunately most decisions about priorities are not made consciously, and are therefore not reflected in the goals you may have created. When you suspect that something is a priority, it may be that it has become urgent,

90 Day Challenge

and urgency can create confusion about whether the activity is a priority or not. When we see something as urgent, we know we cannot wait, and any activity you have planned is set aside because the urgent matter can destroy any plan. There are people living in constant urgency; for them, in their minds, nothing can be planned, and they feel that they work best under pressure in an emergency environment. That may work in some cases, when your job is not to work in a team and you do not have to drag other people into the avalanche of urgency. But if you work with other people, this may be causing constant problems.

Another characteristic of urgency is that it is full of emotions that can be turned into manipulations. This emotional burden puts resources and time at risk, and in many cases it may be that actions are not directed at the objectives.

In order to have objective criteria regarding how to put priorities in order, it is necessary to be clear about the goals to be achieved.

To establish the criteria, ask yourself the following questions:
- Is the activity aimed at an established objective?
- Is there a deadline for completion?
- Is someone waiting for your activity?
- Is the activity required by senior management?
- What would happen if the activity were not completed?

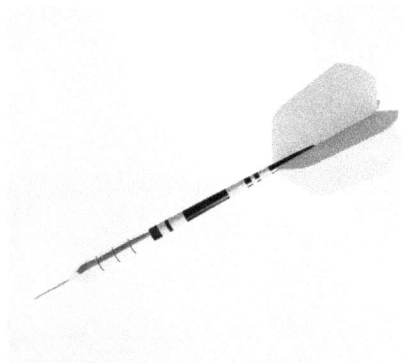

**Goal Setting:** There are different types of objectives, such as personal, work, family. Here we will focus on business objectives and on developing the strategy by which you will identify whether the activities are targeting business objectives, and how to prioritize them.

90 Day Challenge

When considering whether an activity is focused on the objectives, ask yourself the following questions:

- Is this activity directed at your objectives or the objectives of others?
- Is this objective clear and understandable to the members of the organization?
- Is it clear that the goal can be measured and do you know when it must be achieved?
- Is the activity aligned with the objectives of the organization?

**Plan your time:** The key to effective use of time is to _accept what we cannot control and control what we can_. Learning to tell the difference between the two gives us the ability to put our energy and effort on the right track. It is also important to identify time-wasters or, as we call them, time thieves: those activities that not only take away our time and energy, but do not allow us to advance. These time-wasters can be external when created by someone else, or internal when generated by ourselves.

There are many reasons why we waste time and here we list a few:
1. Doing work above your own ability.
2. Tolerating too many interruptions.
3. Completing trivial matters that are of little importance.
4. Working without a plan.
5. Saying "yes" to too many people.
6. Leaving things for "later".
7. Not knowing what to delegate.
8. Lack of self-discipline.
9. Going into detail when it is not necessary.
10. Perfectionism.
11. Frequent changes to immediate objectives.

12. Excessive distrust of people we delegate to.

To end this chapter, I recommend you be your own observer. Through self-observation of what you are doing you will be able to understand where you are wasting your time and take action to:

- Set objectives.
- Establish the activities.
- Set priorities.
- Plan.
- Control and monitor.
- Re-plan, adjust, and improve.

# TIME MANAGEMENT EXERCISE

**SOLUTIONS**

| TIME | ACTIVITY | C. CONT | SUP. C. | DOWNT |
|------|----------|---------|---------|-------|
|  |  |  |  |  |
|  |  |  |  |  |
|  |  |  |  |  |
|  |  |  |  |  |
|  |  |  |  |  |
|  |  |  |  |  |
|  |  |  |  |  |
|  |  |  |  |  |
|  |  |  |  |  |
|  |  |  |  |  |
|  |  |  |  |  |
|  |  |  |  |  |
|  |  |  |  |  |
|  |  |  |  |  |
|  |  |  |  |  |
|  |  |  |  |  |
|  |  |  |  |  |
|  |  |  |  |  |
|  |  |  |  |  |
| **TOTAL HOURS TIME** |  |  |  |  |
| **TOTAL % TIME** |  |  |  |  |

## CHAPTER 11 (DAY 80)

## Change:  How to Motivate and Lead

The only changes you can make in your business are those you can perform at the moment.  Having a goal or desired path in mind is good, but if you do not take action today, change will never happen.  Future, long-term changes do not materialize unless action is taken in the present.  When you speak of changes in an organization, you begin to build a wall of resistance.  The organization tries to implement new processes and procedures and it becomes an uphill battle; not even old procedures keep working, since the environment becomes confusing; some people are paralyzed because they are waiting for "the change".  Moreover, we have heard it incongruously said that some companies cannot afford to make any changes until business improves.

An immediate change has a dynamic effect on your business, your employees, your customers, and most importantly, you.   Many successful businesses implement with their employees the attitude: "adopt, adapt, or get out of the way."

The change is presented as a positive force and creates an atmosphere of "grow with me".

The participation of key members of the organization helps to move your business forward. Sometimes removing employees who are seen as obstacles in the road helps the motivation and enthusiasm of other staff. This can cause several types of reactions; sometimes it may create tension in the team, but if open and honest communication is established between the leaders and members of each team, where they are committed to the pursuit of change and take it as a rule to "adopt, adapt, or get out the way", there should be no resistance, fears, or misunderstandings.

Involve your suppliers and customers in all aspects of your movement for change, and this way you will be able to achieve their support and commitment. Involving suppliers and customers has a double benefit, because it is a way to demonstrate your intention to improve the organization; and you may also be able to get their help in facilitating the process of change, and to be part of your successful "change team".

When speaking of changes, attitude, and motivation, we must think about how you and your organization's leaders can connect with their teams, how to achieve that empathy, that connection in which there is confidence, freedom of expression, and commitment.

**Leadership**

The leadership of the organization is usually centered on a single leader who uses influence and has the power of communication to disseminate changes. This activity usually begins at the top with a strong focus from top to bottom, from strategic management. As we shall see, there are a number of advantages and disadvantages to this approach.

At first glance, this approach appears to be a simple and effective process for deciding on new directions for the organization and getting directives for making changes. This process leads to organizational transformation through the vision of a logical transition that provides reasons for change; creates an emotionally engaging vision that advances by way of process management, training, support, and collaboration; and solidifies the change through a system of measurement and reward that empowers team members.

To succeed, many of these approaches are based on the leader's relationship with the followers. For example, leaders transform through the power to influence followers from the inside; charismatic leaders have the power to influence followers through transformation from the inside out. They inspire at an additional level of personal connection, which includes values management, morality, principles that can be seen as a call or a goal that comes out in the followers' hearts.

Leaders can be more effective when interacting with group members through interpersonal relationships. The actions these leaders must demonstrate range from mutual support, trust, and respect, to loyalty and influence with the group. Sharing social activities among leaders and groups provides a better way to handle the integration of team members and management of rewards, and a decrease in the potential tensions caused by the changes.

When we participated in a change project in a medium-sized organization, the feeling in the atmosphere at the beginning of the project was *"yet another supposed change, and everything stays the same."* This is another phenomenon that may occur at the time of establishing a change project. When an organization has tried to institute change projects and has not completed them, or just mentions changes but does not act on them, either because they did not establish a plan or because they simply could not demonstrate that the change would produce benefits, this can be a boomerang that dramatically returns to hit the organization.

That's why we recommend setting a plan and especially taking the necessary measurements of the elements you seek to change, and establishing a goal. It is not the same as saying that the organization's sales will improve this year; it is saying that sales will increase by 20% in the next three months. It is crucial that you set goals to achieve when starting a process of fundamental change. This eliminates the suspicions of the team participants who feel they are involved in changes where they work more but do not see the benefits.

When dealing with organizational change, the four stages of transformation are: **force, inspire, guide, and implement**.

To manage these four steps, you must use two types of leaders: transformational and charismatic. These types or classes of leadership can be found in two different people; or one person can possess both qualities and know to handle them depending on the circumstances as they arise, so that person can complete the process of forcing, inspiring, guiding and implementing according to the following premises:

1. Transform values, beliefs, and attitudes to strengthen the change actions needed in the organization.
2. Communicate a compelling vision of the future.
3. Develop a strong emotional support for the vision and mission.

Charisma can be only one of a number of possible attributes a leader can have. A leader can also incorporate honesty, optimism, communication skills, confidence, and consideration. Charismatic leaders use their special relational connection, derived from the chemistry of their link with followers. This chemistry allows them to influence emotions and strengthen their leadership in a given situation. However, transformational leaders without charisma can inspire others emotionally through increased interpersonal connection and intellectual attention.

During the stages of **forcing and inspiring** the transformation, a transformational leader who lacks charisma may need to rely on logic, values, and beliefs in order to generate direct interpersonal bonds with followers, rather than using charisma to induce change. During the stages of **guiding and implementing**, the transformational leader would offer more development, support, and training to the followers than the charismatic leader, as well as giving recognition and rewards to others for their accomplishments, creating functional and self-sufficient teams.

With the variety of situations that may arise in an organization and the diverse personalities of leaders and followers, let's take a look at a situation where the organization maintains a culture where there is a limited amount of time to execute the routine activities of the company, and many decisions must be made urgently. Lack of time and urgency may require an autocratic and task-oriented leadership style. In fact, it seems that the urgent tasks can prevail over many other considerations.

Here we suggest analyzing the boss, the subordinates, and the situation or time in order to get the maximum benefit. Factors such as the leader's knowledge, his or her preferred leadership style, and his or her confidence in the abilities of the followers help to provide background on the type of leadership to which the leader is inclined.

Leaders with better relationships and trust developed with their followers have greater influence. However, in a situation where time is limited, the leader must develop the ability to handle situations under time pressure, without losing the power of influence that must be maintained over followers. Efficient management and providing an example through action is the best way to have followers keep their motivation to follow the guidelines.

On looking at cognitive resources theory, and emphasizing how intellectual abilities, experience and relevant knowledge of work can help form a theory of effective leadership, we discover some interesting information: knowledge and intellect are positive qualities of a leader. Though the two meet in a sense, in other theories, we have been surprised by the level of support these characteristics offer to leadership. Having experience increases the level of leadership performance under stress conditions. You can imagine the level of stress that some change management leaders must face. They must be able to direct their followers based on the experience needed to maintain emotional control of stress.

The intellectual capacity of a leader promotes the performance of the group in a positive way when the followers are supporters and the leader is the director, but has no impact on groups that are not supporters. The intellectual leader is seemingly absent in contingency models, because that sort of personality is limited in times of high stress; but it is possible to incorporate the confidence and authority of that kind of leader into this knowledge. The lesson here is that intelligent leaders are very beneficial. They just need to keep a balance in terms of experience and the type of groups and situations they must lead.

## HOW TO DO IT

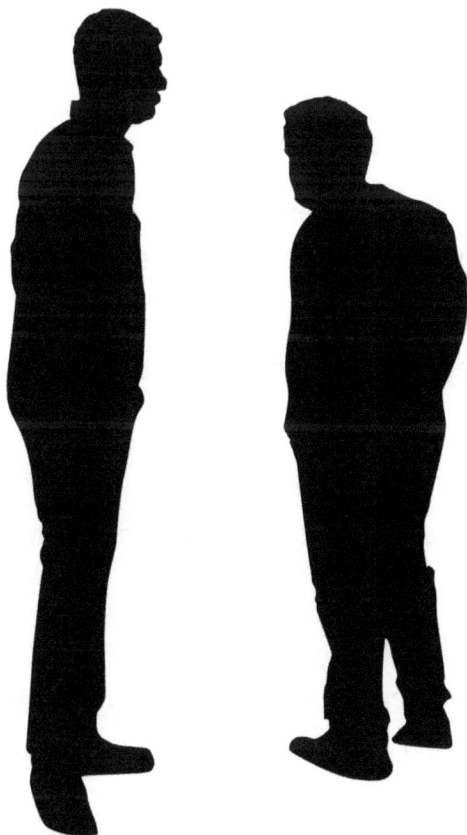

Once you have determined where you want to be, it's time to start making changes. Routine meetings should be scheduled to face each step with your "change team". Focus on achieving short-term goals.

The simple fact that you are here, finishing the 90-day plan, in which you have completed the various tasks and activities the plan gives you, is part of the change you started undergoing from day one. We know there are many responsibilities weighing on your shoulders, but the commitment you have taken on with your organization will not let you step back after starting this process. You already have the information in your hands; the knowledge is going through your DNA; the objectives and goals are determined; you only need to move forward, complete the required actions, and project the passion and enthusiasm that only you can offer your team so that they feel the confidence and commitment to accompany you on this path to success.

First make the visible changes, so that people know you are listening to your customers, employees, and suppliers; that you are ready to take on the challenge of changing the organization supported by your team, and using the leadership techniques needed to turn this process into a pleasant road for the organization, where obstacles are seen as elements of learning, and the strengthening of the processes will ensure the sustainability of the organization.

## SOME PRINCIPLES OF CHANGE AND MOTIVATION

- Don't spend your energy on emotions, but on solutions.
- Don't focus on the problem, but on the opportunities offered by the situation.
- Take responsibility for correcting things, and don't blame others.
- Listen empathetically to others.
- Be open to new ideas.
- Lead a full personal and professional life that is an example of motivation and inspiration for others.
- Lead by example.
- Manage trust and respect as unimpeachable values in the organization.
- Transparency in communication is vital.
- Hire smart people and maintain good communication.
- Promote creativity within the organization.
- Make decisions based on grounds that are technical rather than emotional.
- Be responsible for agreements and manage discipline.

- Publicly acknowledge your team's successes.
- Be consistent in what you say and what you do.
- Enjoy and celebrate each success, and learn from failures.
- Remember that the main commitment is to yourself, and others will feel a commitment to you.
- In critical situations, listen and ask questions first before giving directions.
- See problems as situations that provide opportunities for improvement.

## CHAPTER 12 (DAY 82)

## How to Evaluate and Control Business Risks

It is necessary for any type of organization to know and manage risks in its processes, activities, services, products, and staff. Many people know and talk about business risks, but very few know how to manage them. Risks often seem as if anything can happen, but most people think that nothing will ever happen to them; moreover, people try not to think about risks, believing that if they think and imagine the risks they will appear, as in a ritual where "bad luck" is invoked. These people believe that if they start thinking something will happen to the organization, the chances of it happening will increase.

We can assure you that not thinking about risks does not make them go away. The existence of risk in every activity you do in life is real. And not foreseeing the existence of risk puts you and the organization in a more vulnerable position. The point is that you can minimize, control, transform, and eventually eliminate the risk when it is evaluated, treated, monitored, and managed. Well-handled risk management guarantees a beneficial impact on the probability of the risk's occurrence and materialization, and it doesn't just help to control it. Risk management will improve the organization's strategies and effective decision-making. It will help with change management and increase operational efficiency, as well as providing other benefits such as cost reduction, competitive advantage, better market presence, and even a better image as an organization in the community.

**Principles of risk management**

Risk management is a systematic process that is supported by a number of principles. These principles form the pillars which support the structure of the organization under an internal and external focus. For the design of risk management, it is necessary to know the size of the organization, its nature and complexity, the scope of its activities, and its limitations not only in terms of its internal management but also external aspects that may affect it, whether legal, regulatory, government, financial, social, etc.

For profound risk management, it is necessary to know the governing principles:

1. The design of risk management should create value for the organization, assisting with legal, financial, quality, safety, health, and environmental management, among others.

2. Risk management should be part of the existing organizational processes, and should not be seen as an additional control, but should be immersed in each of the existing processes and activities.

3. When establishing the criteria to be controlled, they must permit easy decision-making by the organization's directors.

4.  There should be a specific focus on managing uncertainties, and how to take action to control them.

5.  Risk management should be designed under a systems approach, where each of the parts is linked and results can be measured to confirm reliability.

6.  Monitor the best information that goes into the processes such as experience, observation, analysis, and expert recommendations, so that the information is dealt with in terms of risk management.

7.  The design must be made to fit the organization, structured by the type and scope of its specific risk profile.

8.  Management should take into account the human and cultural aspects related to the organization, both in the outside environment and within internal management.

9.  The information used in management should be transparent and open so that stakeholders have access to the information.

10.  The risk management system should be dynamic, interactive, and responsive to change.  Keep the information updated, and monitor the constant exchange between events and the information provided.

11.  The organization should ensure the implementation of continuous improvement strategies, based on risk detection, analysis, and implementation of improvement actions.

**Risk Assessment**

This consists of identifying risks, followed by evaluating or classifying them. To create a detailed risk assessment, we will provide the necessary tools for designing your risk management system. Remember that every risk management system is tailored to suit the organization, but what we offer here is a generic model, and the details of adjustment must be developed for you and your team. If you have the chance to get an expert in the area to help you in the use of risk assessment, it is recommended that you do it, because here you are playing with elements of supreme importance to your organization.

The goal of offering you the "**Risk Assessment**" form is to allow you to record information in a table or spreadsheet that will be easy to look at, since you will structure it for processes or activities, thus allowing it to sweep through every area of the organization. Although a simple description of a risk is sometimes enough, there are circumstances where detailed description of the risks may be required in order to provide a holistic view of the evaluation process.

See how interesting it is to be able to weigh a risk, to manage it, and to know which risks are more likely than others and what kind of impact they can have on the organization. Risks can be quantitative or qualitative in terms of their probability of occurrence and their potential consequences or impacts. The organization needs to develop its own methodology for measuring the likelihood of the risk. A simple evaluation method might be to multiply the threat by the vulnerability.

Let's define each term:

**Risk:**   The combination of the probability of an event's occurrence and its consequences.

**Threat:**   The dangerous condition that can cause the risk; determined by its intensity and frequency.

**Vulnerability:**   The characteristics and circumstances that make the organization susceptible.  Vulnerability is composed of exposure, susceptibility and resistance to adaptation to effects.

## RISK = THREAT x VULNERABILITY

TYPES OF THREATS
- Natural disasters (floods, earthquakes, hurricanes, etc.).
- Human (lack of staff, poor maintenance, management error).
- Technology (equipment failure, lack of connectivity).
- Security (physical, personal, financial, social).
- Deliberate or intentional.

Threats can be classified from very low, low, medium, and high to very high, and can be characterized with numbers, for example 1 to 5.

TYPES OF VULNERABILITY
- Lack of knowledge.
- Fraud.
- Loss of assets.
- Loss of staff.
- Theft of products.
- Decomposition of raw materials.

The vulnerability may vary depending on the type of business and process you are evaluating. We have simply listed a few examples so you can have an idea of risk management in your organization.

These can also be classified from very low, low, medium, and high to very high, and can be characterized with numbers from 1 to 5.

**Management of the risk assessment table**

For the design of the risk assessment, follow these steps:

STEP 1: The first column of the table shows the name of the **activity to be evaluated**. You can guide yourself with your list of processes and procedures for the area and select the activities that you are interested in evaluating.

STEP 2: Determine the **nature of risk**. Here is where you develop the possibilities of risks that this activity can incur. You can have more than one type of risk associated with this activity.

STEP 3: The **frequency** with which the activity is performed. Here you should write whether the activity is done daily, weekly, biweekly, monthly, or as often as it is done in the organization. This will help you determine whether the threat is high or not.

STEP 4: Indicate the **threat** presented by this activity as a number, according to the scale determined by the organization.

STEP 5: Indicate the **vulnerability** involved in this activity as a number, according to the scale determined by the organization.

STEP 6: Multiply the number in the threat box by the number in the vulnerability box, and write the resulting number in the **risk index**.

STEP 7: The **type of control** to be applied, whether to minimize the risk, transfer it, tolerate it with controls, treat it to modify its source, or eliminate it. Remember that when the risk index is high, more attention must be paid to the implementation of controls.

STEP 8: Describe **the actions** required to accomplish whatever was determined in the previous box as the type of control to be applied.

STEP 9: The **person responsible** for maintaining risk control and the actions. Here you put the name of the person responsible for controlling the assessed risk.

With the development of this table, you can administer practical and secure risk control that will give you more peace of mind at the moment of any contingency, as well as providing you with a decision-making tool. Developing the entire picture with each of the key activities of the organization may be tedious work, but it is worth the trouble when you and your team look at each activity and visualize the inherent risks that you have as an organization.

**MONITOR THE RISK**

To accomplish monitoring, it is necessary to implement the techniques provided in the list of the principles of risk management, where you take care of management tracking, linking people in the

90 Day Challenge

organization, as well as the control and use of information to generate a continuous improvement system. If you established goals in the action plan that you designed in the risk assessment table, this will let you know what level of risk is involved in a certain activity, and how it has improved over time with implementation of the proposed actions. If you do not see improvements, this justifies the recurring review of the table so that it contains an action or group of actions that will improve the process and minimize or eliminate the assessed risk.

You see how interesting the proper use of this technique is, and the benefits it can give you when you apply a *system of business risk management*. Here we list some of the benefits you will get:

- Creation of risk management awareness in the organization.
- Compliance with legal and regulatory requirements, as well as any customer requirements.
- Continuous business improvement.
- Establishment of a reliable method for decision-making.
- Improvement of incident prevention and management.
- Loss minimization.
- Improved management of leadership objectives.
- Improved trust in employees, customers, and suppliers.
- Improved management of the organization's internal information.
- Increased safety in general.
- Creation of a proactive culture, rather than a reactive culture.
- Improved identification of opportunities and threats.
- Better management of resources.
- Creation of a culture of prevention.

# RISKS ASSESSMENT

| ACTIVITY | NATURE OF RISK | FREQUENCY | THREAT | VULNERABILITY | RISK INDEX | TYPE OF CONTROL | ACTIONS | RESPONSIBLE |
|----------|----------------|-----------|--------|---------------|------------|-----------------|---------|-------------|
|          |                |           |        |               |            |                 |         |             |
|          |                |           |        |               |            |                 |         |             |
|          |                |           |        |               |            |                 |         |             |
|          |                |           |        |               |            |                 |         |             |
|          |                |           |        |               |            |                 |         |             |
|          |                |           |        |               |            |                 |         |             |
|          |                |           |        |               |            |                 |         |             |

## CHAPTER 13 (DAY 86)

### Rules for Negotiation

The tool of negotiation can be used as an ability and a skill in any field, whether at work or in your personal or family life. As an individual, the power of being able to negotiate lets you access many fields and achieve goals based on strategic agreements. When you start a negotiation process, the most important thing is to gain credibility with the person, beyond just getting the agreement or commitment you are seeking. The art of negotiation involves a lot of elements that you should take into consideration when sitting in front of others to initiate the process. It means to be clear in your own mind about the objectives to be achieved and the method to be used for this; but it is also important to know what not to use to achieve the objectives, as this is where we exhaust our resources and where the negotiation process is distorted.

On many occasions this process turns into a power struggle, rather than an attempt to reach the goal of yes. When two or more parties confront each other, the first things to emerge are emotional goals about fighting, controlling, and winning that come ahead of the real aim of the process, to negotiate.

The management of power in bargaining situations will depend on the perception of power by each of the parties; this is to say, it is a relative element that depends on how each one perceives and manages power. In general, power is naturally dynamic and evolves quickly, which can cause stress and tension as it requires a lot of energy.

Studies have found that there are four fundamental objectives to pursue during a negotiation process:

**1. - Create value as much as possible:** This means working tirelessly from the early stages of the transition to identify the potential mutual benefits in all relationships, both those within your organization and in the all-important external relationships that are fundamental to its success. It also means identifying alignments of interest that can help you and those with whom you would like to work, the resources that can provide energy and channel you to achieve the necessary results.

**2. - Capture an appropriate part of the value created:** This means making sure that the agreements reached with other influential players will truly benefit you. After all, you have some important goals you are trying to achieve. Although it is gratifying to help others, we must assess to what extent the help will be beneficial or not. You cannot put your own goals at risk at the expense of helping others. And above all, you cannot help others if they do not want to be helped.

**3. - Build and maintain important relationships:** This means, do not try to force the value in your negotiations so that you harm your relationships. It also means, be careful not to use your influence in ways that could be perceived as selfish or manipulative.

**4. - Reputation:** This means getting a reputation as a tough, creative, and trustworthy negotiator. It also means considering all negotiations performed both inside and outside the organization as opportunities to build and strengthen that reputation. A good reputation is an invaluable asset for a transitional leader. You have to fight to get and keep it in every interaction.

**The stronger your alternatives are, the greater your bargaining power will be, and the less you will need to reach a particular agreement.**

**Negotiating types**

The type of negotiation you will establish depends directly on the stakeholders, the search for agreement, and the interests in play.

**Type 1:** Simple commercial negotiation - when a stranger will make a transaction perhaps just once, and is seeking the greatest benefit for both.

**Type 2:** Mercantile commercial negotiation - when the interests to be negotiated are not just momentary, but may be followed by future transactions and can create value over time.

**Type 3:** Negotiation of values - with others who are not family, romantic partners, or business partners, and where the transaction is not a simple commercial transaction, but establishes values and patterns of honor that may generate future ties and relationships.

**Type 4:** Negotiation of values – with family, business partners, and romantic partners, where there is a burden of emotion mixed with interest, behavior patterns, power, values, cultures, and customs. This type of negotiation requires more attention and dedication when establishing the techniques to be used.

**Classes of Negotiation**

**Integrative Negotiation**

This is based on the negotiators' desire for mutual gains and a high level of cooperation. This kind of negotiation is geared toward respecting the negotiator's goals with the aim that the opposing party will consider the result equally satisfactory. In this negotiation, one seeks to guide the aims of the parties towards objectives of common interest.

Among the features of integrative negotiation are:
- Seeking a climate of mutual trust and confidence.
- Seeking the stability of a negotiated settlement to avoid going back.
- Valuing the vision of the parties' future involving projects, resources, etc.

- Valuing creativity and the search for more dynamic options where the parties work together.
- Managing the values of authority and agreement, fulfilling those established by both parties.

## Distributive negotiation

In this case, weak cooperation is demonstrated between the parties; in some cases there is not even the attitude and willingness for negotiation. Here a particular gain is sought, without regard for the other party. In this kind of negotiation, power in its various forms comes into play in order to take advantage of the parties. Here, when one party wins, the other loses. This is why it is not integrative, but distributive.

In the real world, there are often mixed negotiations, in which an integrative process begins with some indicators of a distributive negotiation.

## Negotiation techniques

**1. Establish the clear objective of the negotiation and the objectives of the parties.** When we are in a negotiation process, it is important to know our own goal ahead of the negotiation's goal, because emotions can lead us astray to fight for things that may not align with our goals or are not worth negotiating.

In life, we constantly live in a power struggle, wanting to be right more than to achieve the goal we're seeking at the time. It's the typical story of two people discussing politics on an issue that may have no value for the purposes of the discussion, but is simply put on the table because negotiator A wants to show negotiator B that his or her political party is better than the other. In the end, both know they are not recruiters for a political party or seeking to change the other's opinion, but they simply unconsciously enjoy a debate to demonstrate the positive aspects of one party and the negative aspects of the other. In the end, if one of them asks him or herself what the purpose of the conversation was, he or she will simply see it was a power struggle intended to prove to each other which was in the right or wrong party.

This situation, like many others, wastes time and energy and causes us to lose friends and acquaintances, to destroy relationships and have family problems simply because the passion of a discussion to demonstrate power leads us to break the harmony of a good productive conversation that leads to the achievement and benefit of both parties.

Knowing our own goal before the goal of negotiation is a basic task that we must do, and in which we can use the following questions to help us put the focus on what we want and on developing the objectives:

- Are your own goals aligned with what you want to negotiate?
- Are your goals only yours or are they the goals of others as well?
- Are your goals measurable and can they be accomplished?
- Are your objectives compatible with the objectives of the negotiation?
- In case you do not establish a negotiation, can you go forward with your goals?
- Can you give ground at the time of the negotiation without affecting your goals?

Answering these questions will help you to determine if your goals are clear and to know a little more about the objectives of the negotiation. Many times the tide of emotions brings us to unknown ports, where things can be relaxed or we can feel the despair of having no map or guide.

90 Day Challenge

On the other hand, we often do not know the goals of the other party with whom we negotiate, and sometimes the other party does not know them either. This is when it can be useful to establish possible objectives for the other party. At that moment, the range of opportunities is opened to establish alternatives that the other party may be unaware of, and that can be the door that opens to a negotiation that is attractive to both parties.

It seems a little absurd to think that the other party may not know his or her goals, but our experience as consultants has shown us that there are high numbers of cases where both parties sit down to negotiate without knowing clearly what their own objectives are, much less those of the negotiation.

Keep in mind that many negotiations can reach this first step when the objectives are unknown and it may be that when you know them, you will clearly understand whether or not it is worth negotiating.

**2. Establish your own benefits and those of the other party.** When the objectives are clear and the possible objectives of the other party have been written down, this is when you begin to access a number of resources, opportunities and alternatives.

The task of opening your vision to observe infinite resources and opportunities is based on breaking the old pattern of always seeing the same way, and understanding that everything we see as a problem is a situation that has a chance to improve. When we use this theory of opportunity for improvement, we will be able to see more resources and alternatives when establishing our own benefits and those of others.

Here, you can apply brainstorming and mental map techniques in order to establish those opportunities you had not seen before, and that the other person may not have seen either.

**ELEMENTS OF NEGOTIATION**

When you enter the game of negotiation, there exists not only your point of view but also that of the other people who come into the game, and you should assess and manage this as well as you can so that you do not deviate from the original objective towards the emotional paths the process could take.

1.  Determine how to handle the negotiation, whether directly, through a mediator, through documents, the legal aspects, the wording of agreements, etc.

2.  Define the interests involved in the conflict and those that are causing tension in the discussion.

3.  Maintain an image of rationality and objectivity, which will bring you power and respect at all times during the negotiation.

4.  Maintain flexibility, to allow a comfortable environment for the parties without the rigidity of not finding options or new roads.

5.  Be able to go outside the context of the negotiation when you see that the original goal is shifting, using diplomacy and authority.

6.  Connect with the core values that define the identity of the negotiators.

7.    Manage the risks and losses involved in the decisions that are being negotiated.  This is a key point to guide the parties.

8.  Highlight the common good.  This implies putting an emphasis on collective benefits and minimizing individual benefits.

For every business person, the topic of negotiation is reflected in daily life, from negotiating a big deal with your best customer to negotiating who makes coffee in the office on Fridays.  It is an issue that can bring peace of mind or stress, depending on your perception; and if you practice these techniques every day, seeking to improve your ability as a negotiator, you will be able to connect much better with people and reach agreements that are beneficial to both the company and your personal life.

## CHAPTER 14 (DAY 88)

## Creativity, Innovation, and Continuous Improvement

There are many ways of defining innovation, ranging from creating new inventions or new proposals to implementing them. It is said that an idea is truly innovative when it is designed and put into practice, and its benefits can be demonstrated. In order to generate innovation in your business you need to know the skills of your organization's members and the guidance and inspiration that the leader can offer.

When we speak of skills, they can be understood to be a reasoned knowledge for dealing with uncertainty; managing uncertainty in a world that is changing socially, politically, and in terms of labor in a globalized society in constant flux. Skills cannot be approached only as observable behaviors, but as a complex structure of attributes needed for performance in different cases where knowledge, attitudes, values, and abilities are combined with the tasks that must be fulfilled in certain situations.

Skills must be seen as complex processes that people put into action, performance, creation, to resolve problems and fulfill the activities of daily life and in the social, labor and professional contexts, contributing to the construction and transformation of reality. They integrate **the knowledge of being, the knowledge of knowing, and the knowledge of doing**, taking into account the specific requirements of the environment, personal needs, and processes of uncertainty, with intellectual autonomy, critical consciousness, creativity, and a spirit of challenge. Skills consist of underlying processes, such as cognitive-affective processes.

Each person is a universe in dialogue with the world, so that a human is a differential sample, is the open and communicating result of the dynamic and interdependent complexity we live in; therefore, skills should be approached as a dialogue between three central axes: *the demands of the labor-business-professional market, the requirements of society, and the management of human self-realization.*

MANAGER

A skill is not an intrinsic characteristic or a separate question from the knowledge acquired through life experience. On the contrary, it is born and grows with a person, with the usefulness of the knowledge and the knowledge of its usefulness. A skill is a vehicle that transports knowledge, and intelligence is the lubricant that facilitates progress; both questions determine the level and performance of the final product resulting, ultimately, in the real skills of people throughout life. The formation of skills is a mixture of balanced forms where the most characteristic ingredients of knowledge try to discover some or many of the hidden flavors (talents, abilities, aptitudes, and attitudes) that have a major impact on your organization's resulting product.

## Knowledge Management

Knowledge management is the learning and activity that allows you to generate, share, or distribute and use the tacit knowledge (know-how) and explicit knowledge (formal) found in a certain space, so that individuals and communities can apply it when they must meet their development needs.

Knowledge has always been considered a factor that promotes the advancement of civilization, and that allows us to solve problems, to adapt to environmental conditions, to manage groups, to impose rules, to face critical situations, and ultimately to improve the living conditions of humans.

At present, the need to increase the dynamics of change and to adapt to flexible working models has led to an increase in the intensive use of information as a key resource for good performance. In turn, this fact increases the use of technology and the development of learning processes as a mechanism to incorporate new knowledge.

In the first case, a difficulty can arise with the incorporation of technology developed abroad or in other cultural contexts from differences between the cultural maturity of the place where it was created and that

of the organization that wants to implement it, which translates into differences in practices. And in the second case, the failure to create a language for change in order to create learning of the new practices these technologies impose causes a consequent resistance to change.

Organizations must produce knowledge, even if acquired from outside; the need to prepare the adaptation of its members forces it to create objects of knowledge, such as transfer methodologies, conceptual models, the design of new skills, the definition of new processes, programs that administer learning and not training, design of fees for skills, study plans based on a skills approach, and the management of knowledge-based processes.

For organizations, knowledge management is the set of elements that describe a certain object or part of reality, which they use to act on this reality with greater efficiency and productivity. The elements range from neutral data, information, and knowledge applied to an object, acquired experience, learned abilities, among others.

The process of constructing permanent knowledge involves active learning to work and to create these elements. In general, this process is generated in the same operative installed contexts and with a status quo that is prolonged in time. It does not involve the generation of adequate space for development and innovation, introduced into the operation, which generates noise and reasonable conflicts for those within the organization who are pressured by the daily production and the challenging effort to generate products and services with the constant changes in environment. Hence it is essential to manage a shared conceptual model which must be changed by the participants.

The volatility of the changes that take place in organizations in the context of the new economy, and the continuous introduction of new artificial intelligence technologies into production and management processes within organizations and companies, have in their turn provoked changes to organizational structures and even to the minds inside them.

The new labor realities are a big challenge and will be from now on; realities that have modified the labor relations contract between organizations, companies, and their members, with emphasis now placed on the development of people's knowledge.

It is not easy to give you immediate answers to this great challenge. Many companies or organizations have opted for the application of a system of labor skills, as an alternative to promoting training and education, in a direction that strikes a better balance between the needs of companies or organizations and their members.

People today are experiencing a process within a new frame of reference which comes from sustained technological development, especially in the new communication technologies, and from the new management models where the basic principles are: **learning to know, learning to do, learning to make, learning to live with others and finally learning to be**; this has a new significance for knowledge management as a new paradigm of the 21$^{st}$ century.

In the administrative context, the information society and the knowledge society are two dimensions of the ongoing process of development, in which human talents stop being passive subjects and become active participants, which facilitate the improvement of production processes and stimulate the introduction of new work skills to take on the most important and unique challenges of the current era, and overcome in this new way fears of failure, of rejection, of criticism, of the traditional patterns of hierarchy, and thus break old mindsets that have created so much damage inside and outside different organizations.

In this sense we can say that **knowledge** is the most valuable asset of any organization in the information society. Thus we speak of the knowledge society and knowledge economy. The competitiveness of firms, and therefore their survival, depends on this knowledge being preserved and used efficiently.

**Hence, knowledge management can be seen as** *the art of creating value from the intangible assets of an organization related to the use of strategic information to achieve business objectives, in order to perform an organizational activity that allows the creation of an infrastructure and social environment so that knowledge can be easily accessed, shared, and created, and is placed within the reach of every employee for your business to be effective.*

**Work Culture**

Work culture requires a new set of cognitive, social, and technological skills, since business organizations have adopted changes in at least two broad categories such as:

**Networking.**  Pyramidal, hierarchical and closed structures have started to be replaced by interactive, open business networks, increasing the decentralization of decision-making to units that gain more autonomy.  Central management assumes a role of defining strategies and evaluating results.  The development of autonomy requires the acquisition of relational, organizational, cognitive, and technological skills.

**Adaptability.**  This means that in organizations there has been a shift from the paradigm based on productivity, in which only standardization and volume are taken into account, representing a rigid model, towards a focus on quality, continuous innovation, and design.  This leads to the notion of a factory that is flexible and adaptable to changing markets in terms of volume and specifications.  In this context, the skills of adaptability, versatility and forming teams arise.

## CONTINUOUS IMPROVEMENT

Competitive conditions mean that a modern company should be constantly changing.  This implies that the new organization is conceived as a dynamic structure, identifying problems and seeking solutions.  This translates into the need for a human resources policy that encourages *systematic training and creativity*.

These new conditions of productivity and competitiveness cannot be attained through limited and reduced training. This has led to substantial modifications to the concept and traditional practices of training, mainly in terms of content and the occupational levels catered to; and it produces a conceptual shift, which changes the relationship of education and training within the educational setting, not only at the university level but also at the business level. Organizations need to be clear about the new conditions of productivity that the business needs and align them with the training of its members.

Thus we need to develop policies for employment training that include the design and implementation of mechanisms that allow workers to better prepare themselves to play a role in a world of constant movement and new working conditions, which supposes the acquisition of basic skills or employability, obtained in formal education as well as corporate training based on practice and experience.

In this respect, we can affirm that the modernization of production based on the criteria of quality, efficiency, competitiveness, and productivity makes it difficult to change the approach from training programs focused on qualifying for a specific job. Certificates or diplomas obtained in this way are beginning to lose value, as what is becoming significant is not the ways in which knowledge was acquired, but the actual results achieved by individuals in their job performance.

In this sense we can say that knowledge management may be necessary to complement the formation of skills developed by members of the organization so that the business can manage its own processes, and can administer and provide services and products in a dynamic environment that easily adapts to market changes. In this way, a culture of continuous improvement is founded within the organization.

## Continuous improvement as a culture

How can we create a culture of continuous improvement in which we can combine the production processes of the organization and the skills of its people? In our years of experience in the world of consulting, one of the most common strategies is to establish processes, procedures, performance indicators and audits, which with daily use create habits that then become organizational culture.

Continuous improvement of the effectiveness of the organization is based on the combination of the mission, vision, objectives, the results of management indicators, the analysis of data, corrective and preventive actions, risk control actions, the control of failures and complaints, and through internal communication processes among members of the organization such as: management review meetings; quality management meetings; operational results meetings; complaint meetings, in which the organization collects information about: measurement reports and data analysis; reports on the results of internal audits; external audit results (customers and suppliers); complaints about product and service quality; minutes of the various meetings; status of corrective, preventive and improvement actions; and reports on the results and effectiveness of actions taken.

At these meetings the organization should deal with the following: review of the behavior (effectiveness, efficiency, potential weaknesses, external effects, opportunity to use better methods, control of changes both planned and unplanned) of processes, and then a review of the different plans of action that have been established. Among the participants, the organization should identify opportunities for required improvement and evaluate priorities, in order to make a decision on the development of improvement projects. The actions arising from the evaluation of the processes responsible must be recorded, along with the names of responsible persons and the implementation dates. The information collected, as well as agreements made, will be input for the organization's continuous and infinite process of improvement and knowledge management.

For you to be able to create this team of creative, innovative people in an environment of continuous improvement we offer the following steps:

**STEP 1:** Keep track of all complaints, claims, and internal problems within the organization.

**STEP 2:** Use the "**Continuous Improvement**" form and place in the first column the name of the process that is affected by the problem you want to improve.

**STEP 3:** Determine the input data that affects the process and determine whether this is the data that can measure the problem.

**STEP 4:** Establish a team of people who will participate as an improvement group to help solve the case.

**STEP 5:** Determine the cause and possible alternatives for improvement; here you can apply various existing techniques for the identification of problems and their causes.

**STEP 6:** Determine what resources you need to implement the proposed alternatives.
**STEP 7:** Begin to perform the proposed actions and assess the impact of those actions.

**STEP 8:** Review and measure the effectiveness of actions and record it. If you find that the actions are helpful, continue doing them; if not, return to step five and again review the causes and new actions.

**STEP 9:** When you see that the problem is improving, document it, and connect it to daily processes as well as any internal training process that is required or should be established.

**STEP 10:** Periodically re-evaluate the situation to monitor its behavior.

Congratulations. Here you have completed the goals of the 90 day challenge that have allowed you to bring all the elements together to develop a method of constant review, and in this way to establish a dynamic organization where changes and continuous improvements produce evolution.

www.90daysolutions.com

**90 Day Challenge**

| PROCESS | INPUT | TEAM MEMBERS | CAUSE | ALTERNATIVES | RESOURCE | DATA MEASURE | MEASURE FREQUENCY | COMMENTS |
|---------|-------|--------------|-------|--------------|----------|--------------|-------------------|----------|
|         |       |              |       |              |          |              |                   |          |
|         |       |              |       |              |          |              |                   |          |
|         |       |              |       |              |          |              |                   |          |
|         |       |              |       |              |          |              |                   |          |
|         |       |              |       |              |          |              |                   |          |
|         |       |              |       |              |          |              |                   |          |
|         |       |              |       |              |          |              |                   |          |

## CONTINUOUS IMPROVEMENT